LIVING GOD'S JUSTICE

LIVING GOD'S JUSTICE

reflections and prayers

COMPILED BY THE ROUNDTABLE ASSOCIATION
OF DIOCESAN SOCIAL ACTION DIRECTORS,
NATIONAL PASTORAL LIFE CENTER
EDITORIAL BOARD

Frank Almade
Suzanne Belongia (Chair)
Joan Jurski, O.S.F.
Jeffry Odell Korgen
Eugene Lauer
Dee Rowland
Jane Villanueva

FOREWORD BY BISHOP ROBERT F. MORNEAU

ST. ANTHONY MESSENGER PRESS
Cincinnati, Ohio

The editorial board respects the use of inclusive language. However, we did not think it appropriate to revise the words of the authors whose prayers follow.

Every effort has been made to trace and acknowledge copyright holders of all the prayers included in this anthology. The editors apologize for any errors or omissions that may remain and ask that any omissions be brought to our attention so that they may be corrected in future editions.

The permissions on pages 199-208 indicate sources for copyrighted works quoted herein and constitute an extension of this copyright page.

Cover and book design by Mark Sullivan
Cover image © istockphoto.com/Robert Trawick
Interior illustrations by Emil Antonucci

LIBRARY OF CONGRESS CATALOGING-IN-PUBLICATION DATA
Living God's justice : prayers and reflections / compiled by the Roundtable Association of Diocesan Social Action Directors ; editorial board, Frank Almade ... [et al.] ; Suzanne Belongia, chair.
p. cm.
ISBN-13: 978-0-86716-742-9 (pbk. : alk. paper)
ISBN-10: 0-86716-742-4 (pbk. : alk. paper) 1. Spirituality—Catholic Church. 2. Spirituality—Catholic Church. 3. Prayers. 4. Justice—Biblical teaching. I. Almade, Frank D. II. Belongia, Suzanne. III. Roundtable (Association : National Pastoral Life Center (U.S.))

BX2350.65.L58 2006
242—dc22

2006021954

CONTENTS

In memory of
Monsignor Philip J. Murnion

PREFACE

Every diocesan social action office director has a moment when she is asked to lead a prayer, sometimes five minutes before a meeting begins! The director will retreat to her office, pull out the "prayer" file, and select the most appropriate prayer for duplication, arriving at the meeting with a minute to spare. As present and former diocesan social action directors, we thought it would be interesting to compile our own "greatest hits," from the files of the members of The Roundtable Association of Diocesan Social Action Directors.

This book is for you: for your own faith development, for those times that you need a social justice prayer for a meeting or a class, and for when you are working on formal prayer services. This is a resource of tried and true material from both wise women and men of centuries past and the most contemporary of authors. The chapters correspond roughly to the major themes of Catholic social teaching, with additional chapters on holidays and holy days and complete prayer services.

During the production of this book, several people made invaluable contributions. Many members of the Roundtable submitted their best-loved prayers. Dan Ebener of the Diocese of Davenport and Chris Loetscher of the Diocese of New Ulm submitted fat envelopes full of spiritual wisdom. Carol Crawford and Marilyn Hite of St. John Vianney Parish in Pittsburgh typed the original manuscript. Aida Rodriguez of the National Pastoral Life Center and Debbye Fihn of the Diocese of Winona provided invaluable help with the most complex part of the project: obtaining permissions! Karen Sue Smith of the National Pastoral Life Center provided pertinent advice about the book's organization and important words of encouragement. We gratefully acknowledge the late Emil Antonucci's contribution of the art that appears in this book—one of his last projects. We thank them and all of those who contributed prayers to this collection.

Rev. Frank Almade, Diocese of Pittsburgh
Suzanne Belongia, Diocese of Winona (Committee Chair)
Sr. Joan Jurski, O.S.F., Diocese of Raleigh
Jeffry Odell Korgen, National Pastoral Life Center
Rev. Eugene Lauer, National Pastoral Life Center
Dee Rowland, Diocese of Salt Lake City
Jane Villanueva, Diocese of Yakima

FOREWORD

Since this is a book about prayer and justice it seems fitting that we begin with a prayer. It is a petition that contains the essential link between our communication with God (prayer) and protecting and promoting the rights of others (justice). It is taken from the Divine Office, the prayer of the church:

> Lord Jesus, you are the true vine and we are the branches: allow us to remain in you, to bear much fruit, and to give glory to the Father.

We have here a summary of spirituality. The metaphor of the mystic vine and branches tells of our intimate connectedness with the Lord. It also makes clear our total dependence upon God. The request to remain in Jesus is what prayer is all about. By raising up our minds and hearts we continually live in God's presence, open to the divine will and the movements of the Spirit. By bearing fruit, fruits that will last, we put our faith into action. A central fruit of the gospel is justice: respecting the rights of all and fulfilling our duties and obligations. If our prayer life is strong and the works of justice are performed with courage and love, then God will be glorified. Such a spiritual life will radiate God's life, light and love, that is, God's grace.

Integration is one of the goals of the spiritual journey. The vertical relationship with God that is nurtured in personal prayer and public worship needs to be integrated with our horizontal relationship with our sisters and brothers. A balanced spirituality is one of *both/and* not *either/or*. In other words, we are to be contemplatives in action. Contemplation is that loving attention as we gaze upon the mystery of God; action is reaching out to others who are in need.

There is another prayer that beautifully captures this integration. It is the Canticle of Zechariah who breaks into song at the birth of his son John. Here is the stanza that brings together both our call to holiness and our call to be a righteous, just people:

> ... the oath that [God] swore to our ancestor Abraham,
>> to grant us that we, being rescued from the hands of our
>> enemies,
> might serve him without fear, in holiness and righteousness
>> before him all our days. (Luke 1:73–75)

The collection of prayers in this volume fosters a balanced spirituality. On the one hand, our attention is fixed upon God, our creator, redeemer and sanctifier. Prayer is about this contemplative gaze. On the other hand, we seek to respond to the Lord's call that we do the works of justice in a broken and twisted world. This volume contains a cry for wisdom to know what to do; it also contains a cry for courage to be of service to all in need.

There is yet a third element in our spiritual life. Not only are we to be people of prayer (nurturing our relationship with God through mutual communication) and a people called to do the works of justice (promoting our relationship with our brothers and sisters) but we also have a relationship with ourselves that needs tending. Prayer and service are incomplete without discipline, mortification, asceticism, that realm of spirituality that sets us free to hear God's word and gives us the energy to serve others. At times we may fail in our attempt to pray and do the works of justice because we lack the discipline needed to raise our minds to God and to reach out to others in need.

Prayer and justice are dependent upon the gift of the Holy Spirit, the Spirit that both prays in us and the Spirit who empowers us to do the works of justice thereby furthering the kingdom of God. Here is a stanza from a Pentecost hymn that is yet another prayer underlying our life of discipleship:

Stay among us, God the Father,
Stay among us, God the Son,
Stay among us, Holy Spirit:
Dwell within us, make us one.

Robert F. Morneau
Auxiliary Bishop of Green Bay
Pastor of Resurrection Parish

CHAPTER ONE

"Just as You Did It to One of the Least of These...
You Did It to Me" (Matthew 25:40)

Prayers and Reflections on the Preferential Option for the Poor

Lord, Open Our Eyes
Kathryn Spink

Lord, open our eyes,
That we may see you in our brothers and sisters.

Lord, open our ears,
That we may hear the cries of the hungry, the cold,
the frightened, the oppressed.

Lord, open our hearts,
That we may love each other as you love us.

Renew in us your spirit
Lord, free us and make us one.

Honor the Body of Christ
Saint John Chrysostom

Do you wish to honor the body of Christ?
Do not despise him when he is naked.
Do not honor him here in the building with silks, only to neglect
him outside, when he is suffering from cold and nakedness.
For he who said, "This is my Body," is the same who said, "You saw
me, a hungry man, and you did not give me to eat."
Of what use is it to load the table of Christ? Feed the hungry and
then come and decorate the table.
You are making a golden chalice and you do not give a cup of cold
water?
The temple of your afflicted brother's body is more precious than
this temple (the church).
The Body of Christ becomes for you an altar. It is more holy than the
altar of stone on which you celebrate the holy sacrifice.
You are able to contemplate this altar everywhere, in the street and
in the open squares.

Have Pity
Saint Augustine

O Holy Virgin,
in the midst of your glorious days,
do not forget the miseries of the world.
Turn a look of kindness on
those who are in suffering
and who cease not to struggle
against the misfortunes of this life.

Have pity on those who love
and are separated.
Have pity on the loneliness of the heart.
Have pity on the objects of our tenderness.
Have pity on those who weep,
on those who fear.
Give us the hope of peace.
Amen.

The Eucharist and the Poor
Mother Teresa

The Eucharist and the poor we must never separate…If we really believe that he, Jesus, is in the appearance of bread and he, Jesus, is in the hungry, the naked, the sick, the lonely, unloved, the homeless, the helpless, the hopeless, then our lives will be more and more woven with this deep faith in Jesus, the bread of life to be eaten with and for the poor.

Prayer to Mary, Mother of Sorrows, Mother of Us All

Jane Deren

Mary, Mother of sorrows,
ease the sorrow of mothers in prison cells
separated from their children.
Grant them courage, strength and hope
so that they might rebuild their lives and their families.
Grant us your compassion
so that we might understand their plight
and support the rebuilding of their lives and families
through just laws, policies and programs.

Come, Mary, Mother of us all.
Move us to see that we are all part of your family.
Help us cherish every child,
respect every mother's dignity,
and tear down the walls that divide us,
so that caring communities might flourish
like May flowers under a blue sky.

A Reflection on Prayer
Archbishop Oscar Romero

The guarantee of one's prayer
is not in saying a lot of words.

The guarantee of one's petition is very easy to know:
How do I treat the poor?
Because that is where God is.

The degree to which you approach them,
and the love with which you approach them,
or the scorn with which you approach them—
that is how you approach your God.

What you do to them, you do to God.

The way you look at them is the way you look at God.

A Constant Attitude
Simeon the New Theologian

Our Lord was pleased to assume the likeness of every poor man and compared Himself to every poor man in order that no man who believes in Him should exalt himself over his brother, but seeing the Lord in his brother, should consider himself less and worse than his brother, just as he is less than his Creator. And he should take the poor man in and honor him, and be ready to exhaust all his means in helping him.

A person is not saved by having once shown mercy to someone, although if he scorns someone but once he deserves eternal fire. For "I was hungry" and "I was thirsty" was said not just of one occasion, not of one day, but of the whole of life. In the same way "you gave me food," "you clothed me" and so on does not indicate one incident, but *a constant attitude to everyone.*

To Care for Others

Lord of Life, empower me
with the guidance of your Spirit
to live in readiness for your coming
in the ways
I feed the hungry,
give drink to the thirsty,
shelter the homeless,
clothe the naked,
care for the sick,
visit prisoners,
bury the dead,
share knowledge of you,
give advice to those in need,
comfort those who suffer,
show patience to others,
forgive one another,
admonish those who need it,
pray for others.
Enliven my heart and
guide my deeds.
In Jesus' name I pray.
Amen.

Prayer for Peace and Justice

God, source of all light,
we are surrounded by the darkness of
the injustices experienced by your people,
the poor who are hungry and who search for shelter,
the sick who seek relief,
and the downtrodden who seek help in
their hopelessness.

Surround us and fill us with your Spirit who is Light.
Lead us in your way to be light to your people.
Help our parish to be salt for our community
as we share your love with those caught
in the struggles of life.

We desire to be your presence to the least among us
and to know your presence in them as we work through you
to bring justice and peace to this world
in desperate need.

We ask this through our Lord Jesus Christ,
your Son, who lives and reigns with you
and the Holy Spirit, one God, for ever and ever,
Amen.

Thoughts on Lifestyle
Pope John Paul II

It is not wrong to want to live better; what is wrong is a style of life
which is presumed to be better when it is directed toward "having"
rather than "being" and which wants to have more not in order to be
more, but in order to spend life in enjoyment as an end in itself. It
is therefore necessary to create lifestyles in which the quest for
truth, beauty, goodness and communion with others for the sake of
common growth are the factors which determine consumer choices,
savings and investments. In this regard, it is not a matter of the duty
of charity alone, that is, the duty to give from one's "abundance" and
sometimes even out of one's needs in order to provide what is
essential for the life of a poor person.

A Letter to the Rulers of the Peoples
Saint Francis of Assisi

Brother Francis, your little and looked-down-upon servant in the
Lord God, wishes health and peace to all mayors and consuls,
magistrates and governors throughout the world and to all others to
whom these words may come.

Reflect and see that the day of death is approaching. With all
possible respect, therefore, I beg you not to forget the Lord because
of this world's cares and preoccupations and not to turn away from
His commandments, for all those *who* leave Him in oblivion and
turn away from His commandments are cursed and *will be left in oblivion*
by Him.

When the day of death does come, everything they think they have
shall be taken from them. The wiser and more powerful they may
have been in this world, the greater will be the punishment they will
endure in hell.

Therefore I strongly advise you, my Lords, to put aside all care and
preoccupation and receive the most holy Body and Blood of our Lord
Jesus Christ with fervor in holy remembrance of Him. May you
foster such honor to the Lord among the people entrusted to you that
every evening an announcement maybe made by a messenger or
some other sign that praise and thanksgiving may be given by all
people to the all-powerful Lord God. If you do not do this, know
that, *on the day of judgment,* you must render *an account* before the
Lord Your God, Jesus Christ.

Let those who keep this writing with them and observe it know that
they will be blessed by the Lord God.

Give Us This Day
Abbey of New Clairvaux

Give us this day our daily bread,
O Father in heaven, and grant that we
who are filled with good things
from your open hand, may never close our hearts
to the hungry, the homeless and the poor.
In the name of the Father, and of the Son,
and of the Holy Spirit.

Help Us
Alcuin of York

God, go with us.
Help us to be an honor to the Church.
Give us the grace to follow Christ's word,
to be clear in our task and careful in our speech.
Give us open hands and joyful hearts.
Let Christ be on our lips. May our lives
reflect a love of truth and compassion.
Let no one come to us and go away sad.
May we offer hope to the poor,
and solace to the disheartened.
Let us so walk before God's people,
that those who follow us
might come into his kingdom.
Let us sow living seeds,
words that are quick with life,
that faith may be the harvest in people's hearts.
In word and in example let your light shine
in the dark like the morning star.
Do not allow the wealth of the world
or its enchantment flatter us into silence
as to your truth. Do not permit the powerful,
or judges, or our dearest friends to keep us
from professing what is right.

From Your Lavish Heart
Alcuin of York

Lord Christ,
we pray your mercy on our table spread,
and what your gentle hands have given us,
let it be blessed by you: whate'er we have
came from your lavish heart and gentle hand,
and all that's good is yours,
for you are good. And we that eat,
give thanks for it to Christ,
and let the words we utter be only peace,
for Christ loved peace:
it was him who said, "Peace I give unto you,
my peace I leave with you."
Grant that our own may be a generous hand,
breaking the bread for all who are poor,
sharing the food. Christ shall receive
the bread we give to his poor,
and shall not tarry to give reward.

Blessed Frédéric Ozanam
Husband, Father, Minister of Christian Charity for the Poor
—Dr. Edward Francis Gabriele

Despite the upheavals of the French Revolution, a huge gulf between rich and poor people still existed in nineteenth-century France. The church had resurgence, but deep suspicions toward it remained. This situation challenged Frédéric Ozanam (1813–1853), and he responded creatively. As a professor at the University of Paris, he showed how the church had served and should defend poor people, and how it had contributed steadily to human progress. He modeled what it means to be a loving husband and father. Perhaps he is best known now for founding the Saint Vincent de Paul Society, whose members worldwide still care for the material and spiritual welfare of impoverished people. Ozanam integrated devout faith, a towering intellect, a loving soul, and active charity; this is why he is considered holy and someone to be imitated.

Morning

Call to Prayer

The rising sun shines on the rich and the poor alike. The spirit of God reminds us daily of our responsibility to care for the poor and those less fortunate because they are the special presence of God in our midst. With Frédéric Ozanam and all the saints, we pray that our service to the poor may be a generous sharing of ourselves, completely stripped of selfishness and condescension.

Praise

Merciful God,
from you comes the true wealth of the heart
and the spirit of generosity.
From of old you reminded your faithful people

that your presence is most clearly seen
in the poor and the disadvantaged.
As Jesus raised the poor,
we celebrate the life and ministry of your servant Frédéric Ozanam.
In his spirit we rejoice that you call us each day
to shed the light of human kindness and love
on those who cry for bread, for mercy,
and for that dignity of life that is at the heart of the Gospel.

Reading (from Frédéric Ozanam)
Philanthropy is a vain woman for whom good actions are a piece of
jewelry and who loves to look at herself in the mirror. Charity is a
tender mother who keeps her eyes fixed on the infant she carries at
her breast, who no longer thinks of herself, and who forgets her
beauty for her love.

Acclamations
Each day God calls us to share with the poor our abundance and love
without counting the cost to ourselves and without regard to our
pride. In joy we pray: *Honor, love, and praise be yours!*

- We adore you, God, whose presence is found most
  graciously in the poor, the lowly, and the have-nots, as we
  pray…
- We are filled with wonder for the power of Christ in our midst
  that raises us to love the unfortunate, as we pray…
- We worship you, God, whose peace must be heralded by our
  deeds of justice in this world, as we pray…
- We are filled with love for your compassion, God, that never
  abandons the poor but hungers and thirsts with them, as we
  pray…

Closing Prayer

Loving God, in the presence of the poor, your love is made supremely manifest. Jesus commanded us to feed the hungry and give dignity to those upon whom the forces of evil have trodden. In the spirit of Frédéric Ozanam, send forth your Spirit. Dispel our fear and quiet our timid heart. Move us to share our abundance with the poor. Do not allow us simply to pity the less fortunate, but to worship your presence in their midst. Amen.

Evening

Call to Prayer

In the growing darkness, we hear poor people cry out to God and us for bread, for shelter, for kindness, and for their promised share of the dignity of being human. With Frédéric Ozanam and all the saints, we pray that God would grant to the Christian community, to every nation, and to every human heart, the gift of greater generosity for the poor, until the forces of poverty are no more.

Thanksgiving

O God, you love the poor and the dispossessed.
When you sent your beloved among us,
Jesus came not into the world of the powerful,
but into the impoverished streets and hearts of his time.
This night your Spirit moves among us once again.
We feel the power of Christ in our midst.
We hear his call to us to feed the poor,
to clothe the naked, to love the unloved.
And our selfishness and sin humbles us.
This night we offer you our repentant prayer of thanks,
knowing that the light of Christ in our midst
is leading us to a new day of Gospel compassion
wherein our heart can be made to overflow in love
for those who hunger for bread, for love, and for dignity.

Reading (from Frédéric Ozanam)
The poor...are there and we can put finger and hand in their wounds...; and at this point incredulity no longer has place and we should fall at their feet and say with the Apostle, *Tu est Dominus et Deus meus.* You are our masters, and we will be your servants. You are for us the sacred images of that God whom we do not see, and not knowing how to love Him otherwise shall we not love Him in your persons?

Intercessions
The poor and the lowly are the intimate friends of God. In the spirit of Frédéric Ozanam, we offer our needs this night, asking in a special way for the spirit of God to make us generous servants of the poor, as we pray: *Keep us mindful of your love.*

- For the church, that we might be divested of every sinful preference we may have for domination, privilege, prestige, and wealth, let us pray...
- For the nations of the world, that every law and structure of society may be founded on mercy and unselfish concern for the betterment of others, let us pray...
- For the members of the Saint Vincent de Paul Society, that their generous service of the poor may be blessed and may be an inspiration to all disciples of Jesus, let us pray...
- For the poor and disadvantaged people, that we may come to love them as Jesus loves us, let us pray...

Closing Prayer
Loving God, in the presence of the poor, your love is made supremely manifest. Jesus commanded us to feed the hungry and give dignity to those upon whom the forces of evil have trodden. In the spirit of Frédéric Ozanam, send forth your Spirit. Dispel our fear and quiet our timid heart. Move us to share our abundance with the poor. Do not allow us simply to pity the less fortunate, but to worship your presence in their midst. Amen.

CHAPTER TWO

"The Lord Takes Pleasure in His People…" (Psalm 149:4)

Prayers and Reflections on Human Dignity

To Love and Know Each Other
Dorothy Day, Servant of God

We were just sitting there talking when lines of people began to form, saying, "We need bread." We could not say, "Go, be thou filled." If there were six small loaves and a few fishes, we had to divide them. There was always bread...

We cannot love God unless we love each other, and to love we must know each other. We know Him in the breaking of bread, and we know each other in the breaking of bread, and we are not alone anymore. Heaven is a banquet and life is a banquet, too, even with a crust, where there is companionship.

We have all known the long loneliness and we have learned that the only solution is love and that love comes with community.

First They Came

Pastor Martin Niemoller

First they came for the Communists, but I was not a Communist, so I
said nothing.
Then the came for the Social Democrats, but I was not a Social
Democrat, so I did nothing.
Then came the trade unionists, but I was not a trade unionist.
And then they came for the Jews, but I was not a Jew, so I did little.
Then when they came for me, there was no one left to stand up
for me.

Hope Is Not the Same as Joy
Václav Havel

Hope is not the same as joy when things are going well, or willingness to invest in enterprises that are obviously headed for early success, but rather an ability to work for something to succeed. Hope is definitely not the same thing as optimism. It's not the conviction that something will turn out well, but the certainty that something makes sense, regardless of how it turns out. It is this hope, above all, that gives us strength to live and to continually try new things, even in conditions that seem hopeless.

Life is too precious to permit its devaluation by living pointlessly, emptily, without meaning, without love and, finally, without hope.

A Prayer to the Holy Spirit
Pax Christi, USA

Come Spirit of God, grant us
> the power to be gentle,
> the strength to be forgiving,
> the patience to be understanding,
> the endurance to accept the consequences
> of holding on to what is right.

Come Spirit of God, help us to
> put our trust in
> the power of good
> to overcome evil,
> the power of love to overcome hatred.

Come Spirit of God, enlighten us
> with the vision to see and the faith to believe in
> a world free from violence,
> a new world where fear will no longer lead us to commit
> injustices,
> nor selfishness cause us to bring suffering to others.

Come Spirit of wisdom and love,
> Source of all good, teach us your truth and guide our actions
> in your way of peace.

Amen.

Remember the Fruits

Found on a piece of wrapping paper in Ravensbruck concentration camp

O Lord, remember not only the men and women of good will, but also those of ill will. But do not remember all the suffering they inflicted upon us; remember the fruits we have brought thanks to this suffering—our comradeship, our loyalty, our humility, the courage, the generosity, the greatness of heart which has grown out of this, and when they come to judgment, let all the fruits that we have borne be their forgiveness.

Eye of Love
James L. Connor, S.J.

When we look at the world with God's "eye of love," we see that: we humans are children of a loving God who invests utmost confidence in us; we are brothers and sisters, not strangers or enemies; all else on the face of the earth is God's gift given to all of us for our common good and our responsible stewardship; the greatest among us is the one who serves the rest; we "find" our lives by "losing" them in love of God and love of neighbor; hostility and hatred are healed through forgiveness, not retaliation and revenge; the world's destiny is decided—it is not in doubt—it is the Kingdom of God in which all tears are wiped away and we rejoice together, as a family around the Banquet Table of the Lord.

A Prayer to Abolish the Death Penalty
Sister Helen Prejean, C.S.J.

God of Compassion,
You let your rain fall on the just and the unjust.
Expand and deepen our hearts
so that we may love as You love,
even those among us
who have caused the greatest pain by taking life.
For there is in our land a great cry for vengeance
as we fill up death rows and kill the killers
in the name of justice, in the name of peace.
Jesus, our brother,
you suffered execution at the hands of the state
but you did not let hatred overcome you.
Help us to reach out to victims of violence
so that our enduring love may help them heal.
Holy Spirit of God,
You strengthen us in the struggle for justice.
Help us to work tirelessly
for the abolition of state-sanctioned death
and to renew our society in its very heart
so that violence will be no more.
Amen.

If You Have Come to Help Me
Lila Watson
Aboriginal Australian Activist and Educator

If you have come
to help me

You are wasting
your time

But if you have come
because
your liberation
is bound up
with mine

then let us work
together.

Prayer for Women
Miriam Therese Winter, M.M.S.

We ask forgiveness
of one another,
woman to woman,
sister to sister.

We ask forgiveness
of one another,
as children of God,
as friend to friend.

Too many times
have we failed to stand
together
in solidarity.
Too many times
have we judged one another,
condemning those things
we did not understand.

We ask forgiveness
for assuming we know
all there is to know
about each other,
for presuming to speak
for each other,
for defining,
confining,
claiming,
naming,
limiting,
labeling,
conditioning,
interpreting,
and consequently oppressing
each other.

We ask forgiveness
for excluding,
withholding,
insisting,
resisting,
the inclusiveness of grace.

Straight With God
Thomas à Kempis

If your heart is straight with God, then every creature serves as a mirror of life and a book of holy doctrine, for there is no creature so little or so vile, that does not show and represent the goodness of God.

Violence
Martin Luther King, Jr.

Violence deepens the brutality of the oppressor and increases the bitterness of the oppressed. It destroys community and makes brotherhood impossible. The ultimate weakness of violence is that it is a descending spiral, begetting the very thing it seeks to destroy. Instead of diminishing evil, it multiplies it. Through violence you may murder the liar, but you cannot murder the lie, nor establish the truth. Through violence you may murder the hater, but you do not murder hate. In fact, violence merely increases hate. So it goes.

Returning violence for violence multiplies violence, adding deeper darkness to a night already devoid of stars. Darkness cannot drive out darkness: only light can do that. Hate cannot drive out hate: only love can do that. The beauty of nonviolence is that in its own way and in its own time it seeks to break the chain reaction of evil. With a majestic sense of spiritual power, it seeks to elevate truth, beauty and goodness to the throne.

Of course you may say, this is not *practical*; life is a matter of getting even, of hitting back, of dog eat dog. Maybe in some distant utopia, you say, that idea will work, but not in the hard, cold world in which we live. My own answer is that humankind has followed the so-called practical way for a long time now, and it has led inexorably to deeper confusion and chaos. Time is cluttered with the wreckage of individuals and communities that surrendered to hatred and violence. We must follow another way.

Eucharistic Prayer for Holy Thursday
World Student Christian Federation

We take bread
symbol of labor, exploited, degraded,
symbol of life.
We will break the bread
because Christ, the source of life,
was broken for the exploited and downtrodden.

We take wine
symbol of blood, spilled in war and conflict,
symbol of new life.
We will drink the wine
because Christ, the peace of the world,
was killed by violence.

Now bread and wine are before us,
the memory of our meals,
our working, our talking;
the story which shapes us,
the grieving and the pain,
the oppressor who lies deep in our own soul;
the seeking and the loving.

And we give thanks
for all that holds us together in our humanity;
that binds us to all who live and have lived,
who have cried and are crying,
who hunger and are thirsty,
who pine for justice,
and who hold out for the time that is coming.

And in this we are bound to Jesus,
who, in the same night that he was betrayed,
took bread and gave you thanks;
he broke it and gave it to his disciples, saying:

"Take, eat; this is my body which is given for you;
do this in remembrance of me."
In the same way after supper
he took the cup and gave you thanks;
he gave it to them saying:
"Drink this, all of you; this is my blood of the new covenant,
which is shed for you and for many
for the forgiveness of sins.
Do this as often as you drink it
in remembrance of me."

This is the death we celebrate.
This is the new life we proclaim.
This is the vision we await.

Before Jesus Was His Mother
Alla Renée Bozarth

Before Jesus
was his mother.

Before supper
in the upper room,
breakfast in the barn.

Before the Passover Feast,
a feeding trough.
And here, the altar of Earth,
fair linens of hay and seed.

Before his cry,
her cry.
Before his sweat of blood,
her bleeding and tears.
Before his offering,
hers.

Before the breaking of bread and death,
the breaking of her body in birth.

Before the offering of the cup,
the offering of her breast.
Before his blood,
her blood.
And by her body and blood alone,
his body and blood and whole human being.

The wise ones knelt
to hear the woman's word in wonder.
Holding up her sacred child,
her God in the form of a babe,
she said: "Receive and let your hearts be healed
and your lives he filled with love,
for This is my body,
This is my blood."

Prayer for an End to Racism
John Bucki, S.J.

Lord, Jesus Christ
who reached across the ethnic boundaries
between Samaritan, Roman and Jew
who offered fresh sight to the blind and freedom to captives,
help us to break down the barriers in our community,
enable us to see the reality of racism and bigotry,
and free us to challenge and uproot it
from ourselves, our society and our world.
Amen.

Martin Luther King, Jr.
Martyr for Human and Civil Rights

—Dr. Edward Francis Gabriele

Martin Luther King, Jr., followed his faith to a course of public, nonviolent, civil protest against the forces of racial discrimination in the United States. His life and work, which ended in his martyrdom, have been a radical witness for subsequent generations who continue to labor for human and civil rights, for equal protection under the law, and for liberty, justice and freedom on behalf of every human being who still suffers discrimination and injustice.

Morning
Call to Prayer
Christ lives in our midst, and so we rise confident that in Christ our life can be made into an instrument of peace and justice. With Martin Luther King and all those who work for human rights, we pray that the spirit of God may make us courageous to take up the graces and crosses that are part of ridding ourselves of violence and discrimination, and that are part of allowing God to pour into our heart the oil of healing and justice.

Praise
Blessed and glorious are you,
O God of all creation,
for the bright dawn of salvation
that has broken into our life.
In the beginning you fashioned us in love
and bid us love one another with the same tender care
with which you brought us to creation.
Despite the ravages of hatred,

you raise up prophets and teachers
to speak your word of peace.
In the fullness of time, you sent to us our Christ
whose life was your presence in our midst.
Crucified for our sake, Christ is among us.
The Savior's word and power is echoed
by many servants such as our brother Martin.
All praise and glory be yours, O God of justice,
for you sustain us this day until that final dawn
when every chain of slavery will be broken
and all your children shall walk in unending freedom.

Reading
Exodus 15:1–3

Acclamations
We remember with joy the life and witness of our brother Martin
Luther King, Jr. Grateful for his life of service, we are refreshed to
enter this day confident that God will give us the courage to give
flesh to the Word of life. In joy we pray: Honor, love, and praise be
yours!

- We glory in you, God of all creation, who has called the
  human race to live in dignity, freedom and peace, as we
  pray...
- We give thanks and praise for the memory of Martin Luther
  King, and for all those who have given their life for justice
  and freedom, as we pray...
- We are filled with wonder at the power of the Word, for
  which women and men have sacrificed their life, as we pray...
- We are thankful for the memory of Martin Luther King, whose
  life of courage has given us hope that human equality is a
  dream coming to fruition, as we pray...

Closing Prayer

God of mercy, we honor the memory of Martin Luther King, Jr., who gave his life that the hope of true liberty might burn ever brighter in this world. By the power of his example, strengthen us to work for justice and freedom for all your children. We ask this through the power of Jesus our Messiah forever and ever. Amen.

Evening

Call to Prayer

Evening is swiftly coming upon us. Despite the advancing shadows, our heart is strengthened by the lamp of justice that burns brightly among us. This day we have celebrated the life and witness of Martin Luther King, whose courage and faith have been a living testimony to the power of God's truth that sets us free.

Thanksgiving

Author of all justice and peace,
when your people walked in darkness
you saw fit to send into our midst
a brilliant lamp that never dims,
a lamp that leads us in every age
into the bright promise of a day without end.
Jesus, your lamp of justice,
crucified upon the wood
 of ignorance, fear, and hatred,
gave his life that we might live,
and showed us how to love one another.
This day we honor the memory of our brother
Martin Luther King, Jr.,
so in love with our Savior
that he offered his life's blood
to be poured out as well

in love of justice and peace.
With Martin and with martyrs for peace in every age,
we give you praise and thanks
for the justice and peace of Jesus that are life.

Reading
Galatians 3:23–29

Intercessions
As we honor the life and memory of our brother Martin Luther King,
let us offer our needs to God, as we pray: *Keep us mindful of your love.*

- For all of God's people, that our life of faith may overflow
  each day into words and deeds that set free all those who are
  held in bondage of any form, let us pray...
- For those who work for justice, peace, and equality for every
  woman, man, and child, that their life may be borne up in
  courage each time that they are made to suffer for their faith,
  let us pray...
- For each of us, that like Martin Luther King we may see the
  invitation to conversion and rid every form of prejudice from
  our heart and mind, let us pray...
- For all those who are the victims of prejudice, hatred, and
  fear, that the presence of Christ may console them, let us
  pray...

Closing Prayer
God of mercy, we honor the memory of Martin Luther King, Jr., who
gave his life that the hope of true liberty might burn ever brighter in
this world. By the power of his example, strengthen us to work for
justice and freedom for all your children. We ask this through the
power of Jesus our Messiah forever and ever. Amen.

Sister Thea Bowman
Minister of Gospel Equality for All

—*Dr. Edward Francis Gabriele*

Thea Bowman (1937–1990), a Franciscan Sister of Perpetual
Adoration of La Crosse, Wisconsin, exemplified what it means to
joyously celebrate the love of God while teaching the gospel of
justice. An African American raised in Mississippi and a convert to
Catholicism, Bowman courageously decided to join this Wisconsin
religious community because the sisters embodied for her the
embrace of gospel equality for all persons. After a celebrated career
in higher education, she turned her tremendous energy and love
toward teaching others the beauty of a multicultural world.
Bowman's love of music, her candid and uncompromising personal
acceptance of all people, and her stirring reminders of the justice
and peace implications of the gospel made an impact on millions of
people, from those on street corners to those worshipping in
cathedrals. Even after being stricken with cancer in 1984, she
traveled throughout the United States and to Africa, spreading the
word of God.

Morning
Call to Prayer
With the coming of each day, God offers the divine splendor of grace
and spreads before us the human family arrayed in rich and
wonderful diversity. The Creator invites us to celebrate in our
diversity the fullness of God's life that binds us as one community.
With Thea Bowman and all workers for equality, we are strengthened
this day to confront the dark forces of discrimination and to open
our arms wide to welcome others as Jesus does.

Praise
God of every race and nation,
in the beginning you fashioned our human nature
and stood over us with love
as the families of the world grew in your sight.
In Jesus you crowned for us the revelation of your will:
that you wish us to love one another
as you have loved us in Christ.
We confess our hardness of heart
and the pockets of fear and intolerance
for people unlike ourselves.
This day your Holy Spirit inspires us
to climb over the walls that divide us
and be bound as one people,
one family of love, proclaiming your glory.
Your love for us in Christ binds us in unity and love.

Reading (from Thea Bowman)
If we reflect together on the specific traditions which we embrace,
our own ideas, values, and convictions are clarified, redefined, and
confirmed; our differences are understood; our commonalties are
celebrated, and we are empowered for life in an ecumenical age and
a pluralistic society.

Acclamations
We celebrate the gift of our unity among the diversity of our human
family. We are grateful for the power of the Spirit, who binds us in
Christ as one people. In joy we pray: *Honor, love and praise be yours!*

- We adore you, God, who has fashioned us as one people
  from many races and nations, as we pray…
- We are grateful for the gifts of all people that give glory to
  the multitude of graces that God holds out for all creation, as
  we pray…

- We honor you, God, whose loving Spirit breaks down the walls of hatred, prejudice, and discrimination, as we pray...
- We are filled with joy for the message of the Gospel that moves us to embrace all people as our sisters and brothers, as we pray...

Closing

God of all creation, you fashioned us in love. You bid us to love one another with the same passion with which Jesus poured out your presence in our midst. In the spirit of Thea Bowman, breathe forth your power of creation and break down the walls of hatred and discrimination. Bind us always in Christ as one people ever tending this world as the garden of your delights. Amen.

Evening

Call to Prayer

Daylight is ending, and the night is coming. Yet we know that from dark corners of the human spirit, forces rob thousands of their security and dignity because they are judged as different. With Thea Bowman and all who work for justice and compassion, we ask God to kindle in our midst the lamp of Christ that strengthens us to work for justice and peace until the coming of the fullness of God's Reign.

Thanksgiving

O God, who rested from your labors on the seventh day,
you have given to our human family
the mission of tending the beauty and dignity of all creation.
You fashioned diverse peoples and races
to witness to the bright spectrum of your loving.
Into our world, you sent your only begotten Son
to speak forth the truth of your loving
that alone is our salvation.

Stretched out upon the cross,
Jesus gave his life for us
that we might learn to love one another
as you have loved us from the beginning.
In the risen Christ,
you gave the greatest gift;
death has been conquered.
In this nighttime you stand by us faithfully,
teaching us in Christ to sacrifice for the good
and to hope for the promised glory,
especially for those the world has robbed
of their dignity as your daughters and sons,
your messengers of grace until the day of your coming.
Your love alone binds us as your family.

Reading (from Thea Bowman)
[People often ask me how I keep going.] My early training is part of
the ethic that enables me to do that. Old people in the black
community taught us that we should serve the Lord until we die. We
can even serve the Lord on our deathbeds or in any circumstances in
life. If we have faith, hope and love we can pass it on.

Intercessions
God has created us to live in harmony and love and to bind all people
into the one family of grace. With Thea Bowman and all those who
work for equal rights, we bring our needs before the God of all
graces, as we pray: *Keep us mindful of your love.*

- For all Christians, that our efforts to build up the one Body of
  Christ may be a witness to all of the unity of the human
  family, let us pray…
- For all those who work for racial and human equality, that
  their hands may always be strengthened by the Holy Spirit,
  let us pray…

- For all those who oppress others because of human hatred, that the Spirit may lead them to break free from their bondage and sin, let us pray...
- For those who suffer at the hands of human hatred and bigotry, that our loving may be God's balm for their life, let us pray...

Closing Prayer

God of all creation, you fashioned us in love. You bid us to love one another with the same passion with which Jesus poured out your presence in our midst. In the spirit of Thea Bowman, breathe forth your power of creation and break down the walls of hatred and discrimination. Bind us always in Christ as one people ever tending this world as the garden of your delights. Amen.

CHAPTER THREE

"The Cries of the Harvesters Have Reached the Ears of the Lord" (James 5:4)

Prayers and Reflections on the Dignity of Work
and the Rights of Workers

Remember the Immigrant
Interfaith Worker Justice

Leader: We serve a God who directs us to care especially for those most vulnerable in society. Our Scriptures tell us of God's special concern for the "alien" or the "stranger," or as more contemporary translations say—the immigrant.

All: For the Lord our God is God of gods and Lord of lords, the great God, mighty and awesome, who shows no partiality and accepts no bribes. God defends the cause of the orphan and the widow, and loves the immigrant, giving the immigrant food and clothing. And we are to love those who are immigrants, for God's people were immigrants in Egypt. (Deuteronomy 10:17–19)

Leader: We ask God to open our eyes to the struggles of immigrant workers, for we know that

All: We must not take advantage of a hired worker who is poor and needy, whether the worker is a resident or immigrant living in our town. We must pay the worker the wages promptly because the worker is poor and counting on it. (Deuteronomy 24:14)

Leader: God's desire is that those who build houses may live in them,

All: And that those who plant may eat. (Isaiah 65:22)

Leader: And yet we know this is not possible for many in our midst.

All: We know of: farmworkers who cannot feed their families; construction workers who have no homes; nursing home workers who have no health care; restaurant workers who could not afford a meal in the restaurant.

Leader: We know that too many immigrant workers among us are not receiving the fruits of their labor, nor the justice required by the courts.

All: God charges our judges to hear disputes and judge fairly, whether the case involves citizens or immigrants. (Deuteronomy 1:16)

Leader: But our laws do not adequately protect immigrants. Our legal and social service programs exclude many immigrants. Our education programs undervalue immigrant children.

All: God tells us that the community is to have the same rules for citizens and for immigrants living among us. This is a lasting ordinance for the generations to come. Citizens and immigrants shall be the same before the Lord. (Numbers 15:15)

Leader: When an immigrant lives in our land,

All: We will not mistreat him or her. We will treat an immigrant as one of our native born. We will love an immigrant as ourselves, for God's people were once immigrants in Egypt. (Leviticus 19:33–34)

Leader: To those who employ immigrant workers, we lift up God's command:

All: Do not oppress an immigrant. God's people know how it feels to be immigrants because they were immigrants in Egypt. (Exodus 23:9)

Leader: And a special word to those who employ immigrant farm workers:

All: Make sure immigrants get a day of rest. (Exodus 23:12)

Leader: To those who craft our immigration laws and policies, we lift up God's command:

All: Do not deprive the immigrant or the orphan of justice, or take the cloak of the widow as a pledge. Remember that God's people were slaves in Egypt and the Lord our God redeemed them from there. (Deuteronomy 24:17–18)

Leader: To all of us who seek to do God's will, help us to:

All: Love one another as God has loved us. Help us to treat immigrants with the justice and compassion that God shows to each of us.

Christmas Day Litany
Interfaith Worker Justice

Reader: We offer our prayers to God, who gifted us with compassion in the person of Jesus, who deemed us co-creators with God, and who blesses the labor of all. Compassionate God, make us mindful of the abundant gifts we receive from the labor of many in this season of joy.

All: Compassionate God, make us mindful of the gifts we receive from the labor of many.

Reader: For workers in fields, food plants, restaurants and grocery stores, who raise and prepare the food we enjoy, let us pray:

All: Compassionate God, make us mindful of the gifts we receive from the labor of many.

Reader: For all those who work in nursing homes, providing care and services for those we love, may they receive affordable health benefits for themselves and their families, let us pray:

All: Compassionate God, make us mindful of the gifts we receive from the labor of many.

Reader: For all employers, especially in toy and clothing companies, that they provide a just work environment that does not rely upon the labor of children, let us pray:

All: Compassionate God, make us mindful of the gifts we receive from the labor of many.

Reader: For all employees, that they may receive a living wage to provide for their families, let us pray:

All: Compassionate God, make us mindful of the gifts we receive from the labor of many.

Reader: For retail workers, that in this season of giving and generosity, face long hours, low wages, and anxious shoppers, let us pray:

All: Compassionate God, make us mindful of the gifts we receive from the labor of many.

Reader: For all of us who shop and buy goods, may we have the courage to say "NO!" to goods produced in sweatshops, where women, men and children earn only pennies a day and work in unsafe conditions, let us pray:

All: Compassionate God, make us mindful of the gifts we receive from the labor of many.

Reader: For all workers, that in this season of giving and generosity, they will receive affordable health benefits for themselves and their families, let us pray:

All: Compassionate God, make us mindful of the gifts we receive from the labor of many.

Reader: For those who are without any or enough work, especially in this season of abundance, may they also reap the benefits of our "good" economy, let us pray:

All: Compassionate God, make us mindful of the gifts we receive from the labor of many.

Reader: Compassionate God, let our hearts and minds be opened in this season of light. As we celebrate the gifts of Your loving presence, may we never stop working to build Your reign here on earth so that all of creation knows and experiences Your justice, joy and peace.

All: Amen.

Bountiful Harvest

Father Ermolao Portella, Colombia

Lord Jesus,
in images of farming and rural life
you announced your gospel to the poor.

We pray for rural men and women,
especially for those who work hard in the fields.

Give us the strength of your Spirit to be witnesses
and collaborators of the creative providence.

May we always sow in ourselves and in our families
the holiness and hope of Christian life,
with the same zeal with which we cultivate our land.

Bless the daily efforts of farmers and farm workers.
Let all recognize the dignity of their labor.

Raise from among us men and women
at the service of the gospel,
sisters and brothers to announce unceasingly
your love for this world that is your own field and farm.

We give you glory forever and ever.

Excerpt From Labor Day Mass
Cardinal John O'Connor

[This]… must be the hallmark of organized labor in our country. We must do everything well. We must do everything as we are required to do to the very best of our ability. We must treat people as made in the Image and Likeness of God, everyone without exception: employer, employee, rich, poor, whatever color, whatever ethnic background, men and women [must be treated as human persons made in the Image and Likeness of God].

That is the beginning of true collective bargaining in justice. We must recognize the sacredness of every human person....This is ultimately what unionism and collective bargaining is about — to try to bring justice, but justice to all, not just either to the "haves" or to the "have nots," justice to everybody.

The Gift of Work

Caritas Nicaragua

Thank you, Lord, for permitting me to live this new day!
Thank you all the more for permitting me to begin this workday.

I ask you, Lord, to give me the strength of your blessing:
to share efforts with my fellow workers,
to recognize my mistakes,
and, this very day, to amend
whatever could hamper my work of tomorrow,
be it alone or in collective responsibilities.

I ask you, my Lord, to be the worker here
and, by means of my work instruments,
prepare for the magnificence of your return,
with the harmony of duty fulfilled,
with patience in the midst of impatience,
with community in the face of contempt,
with joy where there has been sadness.

I ask you, Lord, for work for those who do not have it,
for strength of will in all your children
so that they can share this blessing.
In turn, Lord, I offer you little:
simply each moment of this day as it comes.

Let us be your sons and your daughters,
with our heads held high in material work,
and, afterwards, let us prepare to rest in your embrace
and await the coming of a new day to glorify you:
today, tomorrow and always, until our lives be your life.

Prayer to St. Joseph, Patron of Workers
Jane Deren

St. Joseph, Patron of Workers,
Help us to respect the dignity of all workers.
Help us to learn about and to care about
Workers who do not have fair wages, just benefits, safe working
environments.
Help us to raise our voices for justice for workers.
Help us to ask our government and our representatives
To develop policies that create jobs with dignity.

You taught your son
The value of work and the joy of work well done.
Teach us these lessons.
Guide us in our own work
And in the work of justice we are all called to participate in.
Renew our strength and commitment
Each day as we face the work ahead
As we labor for the common good of all.
Amen.

Prayer to the Holy Family, Especially for Those Seeking Employment

Archbishop Jerome G. Hanus, O.S.B.

Lord Jesus Christ, we call upon You as our Savior and ask that You look kindly upon us, our families, and our community. We acknowledge that it is in Your Name alone that we are saved.

In this time of stress, give us the consoling awareness of Your presence, through the spiritual gifts of courage and patience.

Mary, Mother of Christ and model Disciple, you accepted the angel's word asking you to bear Christ. Help us to bear the Christian message of support to our neighbors in need.

Saint Joseph, patron of all workers, intercede to God for us, especially those of us who need employment.

As you sustained the Holy Family by the work of your hands, help us and those who can provide us with work, so that together we may build a society where all are respected and honored as creatures of God and brothers and sisters to one another.

To God, Creator and Provider, be all honor and glory, now and forever. Amen.

Prayer to Saint Isidore
National Catholic Rural Life Conference

Let us pray.
Grant, O Lord,
that through the intercession
of blessed Isidore the farmer,
we may follow his example of patience and humility.
May we walk faithfully in his footsteps
that in the evening of life
we may be able to present to you
an abundant harvest of merit and good works,
for you are the one God
now and forever.
Amen.

Prayer of the Christian Farmer
National Catholic Rural Life Conference

O God, source and giver of all things,
who manifests Your infinite majesty, power and goodness in the
earth about us,
we give You honor and glory.
For the sun and the rain,
for the manifold fruits of our fields,
for the increase of our herds and flocks we thank You. For the
enrichment of our souls with divine grace, we are grateful.
Supreme Lord of the harvest
graciously accept us and the fruits of our toil
in union with Christ Your Son, as atonement for our sins,
for the growth of Your Church, for peace and charity in our homes,
for salvation to all. Amen.

Doers, Not Just Hearers: A Labor Day Prayer Service
Interfaith Worker Justice

Leader: As we gather together this Labor Day weekend, we recognize that we serve a God who has set forth guidelines for treatment of workers and immigrants. Living a life acceptable to God requires good relationships with God and with our neighbors.

All: Every generous act of giving, with every perfect gift, is from above. (James 1:17)

Leader: You call us to treat our neighbors as we want to be treated ourselves.

All: We want to be doers of the word, and not merely hearers who deceive themselves. (James 1:22)

Leader: We know that You want all workers to be treated with respect and dignity.

All: We want wages and benefits that can raise our own families and so we want it for others as well.

Leader: For if any are hearers of the word and not doers, they are like those who look at themselves in a mirror; (James 1:23)

All: For they look at themselves and, on going away, immediately forget what they were like. (James 1:24)

Leader: But those who look into the perfect law, the law of liberty, and persevere,

All: Being not hearers who forget but doers who act—they will be blessed in their doing. (James 1:25)

Leader: When we hear about janitors seeking better wages and benefits for their families,

All: Help us be doers who act. Help us seek justice for janitors.

Leader: When we hear about health care workers and home care workers who cannot afford health care for their own families,

All: Help us be doers who act. Help us seek justice for health care and home care workers.

Leader: When we hear about retail workers who can only work part-time so they are excluded from benefits,

All: Help us be doers who act. Help us seek justice for retail workers.

Leader: When we hear about farmworkers working long hours for low pay, sleeping in cramped housing or on the ground,

All: Help us be doers who act. Help us seek justice for farmworkers.

Leader: When we think about those whom we or people we know employ to watch our children,

All: Help us be doers who act. Help us seek justice for child care workers.

Leader: When we hear about and see the immigrants in our nation who often toil in the hardest jobs, pay taxes, and yet often have no path to become citizens,

All: Help us be doers who act. Help us seek justice for immigrant workers.

Leader: When we hear of loyal employees who have lost their jobs due to no fault of their own,

All: Help us be doers who act. Help us seek justice for laid off and unemployed workers.

Leader: We know that many of our clothes and children's toys are made in sweatshops. Too often "cheap" becomes more important than "just."

All: Help us be doers who act. Help us seek justice for sweatshop workers.

Leader: Help us to remember that work is a gift of God and that each worker is created in the image of God.

All: Oh God who created each one of us, who allows us to work, we give thanks for this Labor Day. We ask You to be with all those who work and are not paid wages to sustain their families. We ask Your special blessing on immigrant workers and those looking for work. Forgive us when we purchase goods made in sweatshops. Help us to seek justice for all workers. Help us be doers who act. Amen.

CHAPTER FOUR

"If One Suffers, All Suffer" (1 Corinthians 12:26)

Prayers and Reflections on Solidarity

The Call to Community
Henri Nouwen

By ceasing to make our individual differences a basis of competition and by recognizing these differences as potential contributions to a life together, we begin to hear the call to community.

In and through Christ, people of different ages and lifestyles, from different races and classes, with different languages and education, can join together and witness to God's compassionate presence in our world.

There are many common-interest groups, and most of them seem to exist in order to defend or protect something. Although these groups often fulfill important tasks in our society, the Christian community is a different nature.

When we form a Christian community, we come together not because of similar experiences, knowledge, problems, color, or sex, but because we have been called together by the same Lord.

Only God enables us to cross the many bridges that separate us; only God allows us to recognize each other as members of the same human family; and only God frees us to pay careful attention to each other.

This is why those who are gathered together in community are witnesses to the compassionate Lord. By the way they are able to carry each other's burdens and share each other's joys, they testify to God's presence in our world.

Night Prayer
Saint Augustine

O watch, dear Lord,
with those who wake,
or watch, or weep tonight.
Give your angels charge over those who sleep.
Tend your sick ones, O Lord Jesus Christ.
Rest your weary ones.
Bless your dying ones.
Soothe your suffering ones.
Pity your afflicted ones.
Shield your joyous ones.
And all for your love's sake.

Prayer for Troubled Times
Barbara Blossom, for the Sisters of Charity of Bronx, New York

O God, in these troubled, uncertain times, we commit ourselves to peace. We remember that each thought has the power to inspire action, and that the actions we take can transform the lives of all those around us, all those whom they encounter, and ultimately, the world.

We will not make room in our hearts for hatred and intolerance. Instead, we live in joy and wonder, marveling at Your beautiful creation, especially our sisters and brothers from lands near and far.

We ask You for strength, vision, and perseverance to reject violence in all of its forms as we lovingly work towards justice for all of Your children.

We trust in Your ways, dear God, and we ask You to inspire us as individuals, leaders, and nations to create a glorious community that embraces and celebrates life.

The Prayer of the Refugee
Jesuit Relief Services, Australia

Lost in the tempests out on the open seas,
our small boats drift.
We seek for land during endless days and endless nights.

We are the foam,
floating on the vast ocean.
We are the dust,
wandering in endless space.
Our cries are lost in the howling wind.

Without food, without water,
our children lie exhausted
until they cry no more.
We thirst for our land,
but are turned back from every shore.

Our distress signals rise and rise again,
but the passing ships do not stop.
How many boats have perished?
How many families lie beneath the waves?

Lord Jesus, do you hear the prayer of our flesh?
Lord, do you hear our voice from the abyss of death?

O solid shore, we long for you!
We pray for humankind to be present today!
We pray that hope be given us today,
from any land.
Amen.

Breath of God, Breathe on Us

O God, the source of our common life,
when we are dry and scattered,
when we are divided and alone,
we long for connection, we long for community.
Breath of God, breathe on us.

With those we live beside,
who are often strange to us,
whom we may be afraid to approach,
yet who have riches of friendship to share,
we long for connection, we long for community.
Breath of God, breathe on us.

With those we have only heard of,
who see with different eyes,
whose struggles we try to imagine,
whose fierce joy we wish we could grasp,
we long for connection, we long for community.
Breath of God, breathe on us.

With those we shall never know,
but whose lives are linked with ours,
whose shared ground we stand on,
and whose common air we breathe,
we long for connection, we long for community.
Breath of God, breathe on us.

When we are dry and scattered,
when we are divided and alone,
when we are cut off from the source of our life,
open our graves, O God,
that all your people may be free to breathe,
strong to move,
and joyful to stand together
to celebrate your name.
Amen.

Spirit of God
Catholic Agency for Overseas Development, United Kingdom

Spirit of God,
you are the breath of creation,
the wind of change
that blows through our lives,
opening us up to new dreams and new hopes,
new life in Jesus Christ.

Forgive us our closed minds
which barricade themselves
against new ideas,
preferring the past
to what you might want to do through us tomorrow.

Forgive our closed eyes
which fail to see the needs of your world,
blind to opportunities of service and love.

Forgive our closed hands
which clutch our gifts and our wealth
for our own use alone.

Forgive us our closed hearts
which limit our affections to ourselves
and our own.

Spirit of new life,
forgive us and break down
the prison walls of our selfishness,
that we might be open to your love
and open for the service of your world,
through Jesus Christ our Lord. Amen.

Come Holy Spirit and Show Us What Is True

In a world of great wealth
where many go hungry
and fortunes are won and lost
by trading in money,
come, Holy Spirit, and show us what is true.

In a world of great knowledge
where many die in ignorance
and every piece of information
has a price in the market-place,
come, Holy Spirit, and show us what is true.

In a world of easy communication,
where words leap between continents
and we expect to see a picture
to illustrate each item of the news,
come, Holy Spirit, and show us what is true.

In a Church which speaks a thousand accents,
divided over doctrine, creed, and ministry,
more anxious for itself than for the Gospel,
come, Holy Spirit, and show us what is true.

In a Church touched by the flame of Pentecost,
moved to generous sacrifice and costly love,
interpreting the will of God with new insight,
come, Holy Spirit, and show us what is true.

Making Room at the Table
Carole Garibaldi Rogers and Mary Ann Jeselson

O loving God, you nourish and sustain us.
We thank you for the gift of food,
which nourishes life.
You continue to be with us
in so many wonderful and marvelous ways,
nourishing and sustaining us always
with food that gives life to all the aspects of our being.
Help us to use the many ways
in which you nourish us
as sources of unity and life
for all of your people.
Allow us to grow in sensitivity
to the plight of those who are hungry,
alone, frightened, shut out, uninvited,
unwelcome.

A Children's Prayer

We pray for children who put chocolate fingers everywhere, who like to be tickled, who stomp in puddles and ruin their new pants, who sneak Popsicles before supper, who erase holes in math workbooks, who can never find their shoes.

And we pray for those who stare at photographers from behind barbed wire, who can't bound in the street in a new pair of sneakers, who never go to the circus, who live in an X-rated world.

We pray for children who bring us sticky kisses and fistfuls of dandelions, who sleep with the dog and bury the goldfish, who hug us in a hurry and forget their lunch money, who cover themselves with Band-Aids and sing off-key, who squeeze toothpaste all over the sink, who slurp their soup.

And we pray for those who never get dessert, who have no safe blanket to drag behind them, who watch their parents watch them die, who can't find any bread to steal, who don't have any rooms to clean up, whose pictures aren't on anybody's dresser, whose monsters are real.

We pray for children who spend all their allowances before Tuesday, who throw tantrums in the grocery store and pick at their food, who like ghost stories, who shove dirty clothes under the bed and never rinse the tub, who get visits from the tooth fairy, who don't like to be kissed in front of the car-pool, who squirm in church and scream in the phone, whose tears we sometimes laugh at, and whose smiles can make us cry.

We pray for children who want to be carried and for those we never give up on and for those who don't get a second chance. For those we smother . . . and for those who will grab the hand of anybody kind enough to offer it.

Prayer of the Second Vatican Council

This prayer was used before every session of the Second Vatican Council.

We stand before you, Holy Spirit,
conscious of our sinfulness,
but aware that we gather in your name.

Come to us, remain with us,
and enlighten our hearts.

Give us light and strength
to know your will,
to make it our own,
and to live it in our lives.

Guide us by your wisdom,
support us by your power,
for you are God,
sharing the glory of Father and Son.

You desire justice for all:
enable us to uphold the rights of others;
do not allow us to be misled by ignorance
or corrupted by fear or favor.

Unite us to yourself in the bond of love
and keep us faithful to all that is true.

As we gather in your name
may we temper justice with love,
so that all our decisions
may be pleasing to you,
and earn the reward
promised to good and faithful servants.

You live and reign with the Father and the Son,
one God, forever and ever. Amen.

Prayer for Women Everywhere
B. D'Arcy

With Miriam, who with Moses and Aaron
led the people of Israel out of Egypt;
with Deborah, who judged the people of Israel
in truth and righteousness;
with Ruth, who was an example of faithfulness;
with Mary Magdalen, who first
brought the good news of the resurrection;
with Phoebe, deacon and leader of the early Church;
with Priscilla, who labored with Aquila
in the service of Christ;
with Dorcas, who spent herself doing good
and helping the poor;
with Mary the mother of Jesus,
who said "yes" with no holding back.

With these, our sisters,
We pray for women everywhere who see
their families divided,
their children sad;
we pray for women who against all the odds
create a good place
for their families to live in;
we pray for women who,
when tempted to give up,
find new strength from their sisters
and go on.

Amen.

God, Food of the Poor
Workers in Community Soup Kitchens in Lima, Peru

God, food of the poor;
Christ, our bread,
give us a taste of the tender bread from your creation's table;
bread newly taken from your heart's oven,
food that comforts and nourishes us.
A loaf of community that makes us human,
joined hand in hand, working and sharing.
A warm loaf that makes us a family;
sacrament of your body,
your wounded people.

On Hospitality
Kathleen Norris

We think of monks as being remote from the world, but St. Benedict, writing in the sixth century, notes that a monastery is "never without guests" and admonishes monks to "receive all guests as Christ." Monks have not been slow to recognize that such hospitality, while undoubtedly a blessing, can create burdens for them. A story said to originate in a Finnish monastery has an older monk telling a younger one: "I have finally learned to accept people as they are. Whatever they are in the world, a prostitute, a prime minister, it is all the same to me. But sometimes I see a stranger coming up the road and I say, 'Oh, Jesus Christ, is it you again?'"

The Women Martyrs of El Salvador
Lives Given in Love

—*Dr. Edward Francis Gabriele*

Lay missioner Jean Donovan, Maryknoll sisters Ita Ford and Maura Clark, and Ursuline sister Dorothy Kazel—the names of these women and their brutal martyrdom are etched into the heart of believers. These missionaries in El Salvador worked among the poorest of people, touching the lives of the poor with the peace that can only spring from faith in Jesus. For their efforts, they were raped and murdered. The age of martyrs has not ended. These women lost their lives because they sought, like Jesus, to heal, to teach the Good News, and to free the captive. The forces of evil cannot tolerate such goodness. As in the early church, memory of these witnesses has stirred others to take their place in the struggle for peace and justice.

Morning
Call to Prayer
As the light of a new day enters our life, the spirit of God calls us to spread the Gospel. Each day we realize that our commitment in Christ demands that we set our hands to the plow of justice until that final day when the fullness of justice will flower. With Jean Donovan, Dorothy Kazel, Maura Clark, and Ita Ford, we pray for the coming of the day of peace that is heralded by our works for justice in this time and in all places where God's will takes us.

Praise
Foundation of every human hope,
in the original darkness of the abyss,
amid the pangs of your labor of love,
you gave birth to us in your image
to be a people of justice and peace.

This day, your brilliant Son of justice
spreads the light of the Gospel before our eyes,
that we might see again the wondrous vision of your love
and be moved in strength to deeds of mercy and compassion.
You open our heart to see your poor
and bid us open our hands to feed them
with bread and dignity.
This day you draw us to love you in the poorest of all
and to feed one another as you have fed us.

Reading (from Jean Donovan)
There's one thing I know, that I'm supposed to be down here, right
now.... You can contribute a lot and make a big difference in the
world if you realize that the world you're talking about might be very
small—maybe one person, or two people. And...if you can find a
place to serve, you can be happy.

Acclamations
With love we call to mind the witness of martyrs of every time and
place. In the spirit of their generosity, we grasp the challenge of
Gospel living on this day. In joy we pray: *Honor, love, and praise be
yours!*

- We adore you, God, who has spread before us the Gospel
  feast of justice and peace for all people, as we pray...
- We are grateful for the vocation of mercy and compassion
  that is given to us in baptism, as we pray...
- We honor you, God, whose justice demands that we confront
  the forces of oppression and evil in every corner of human
  life, as we pray...
- We are filled with joy for the presence of the Spirit wisdom, in
  whose birthing we are made bold for the service of others, as
  we pray...

Closing

O God of justice, with Maura Clark, Ita Ford, Dorothy Kazel, and
Jean Donovan we celebrate the message of the Gospel that sets free
the captives of our world. Make us living witnesses to the freedom of
Christ until that day when the blood of the martyrs will flower with
the fullness of your peace. We ask this as all things through Jesus our
Messiah forever and ever. Amen.

Evening

Call to Prayer

As this day draws to a close, we join with the women martyrs of El
Salvador to pray for the final scattering of the darkness of
oppression in every corner of the world. In our midst is burning the
lamp of justice, the living presence of Jesus Christ, who lights our
pathways and leads us to serve only the Gospel of peace and justice.
The light of Christ warms us with hope and strength to meet with
hope the terrors of the night that threaten the poor and the lowly.

Thanksgiving

God of all compassion,
you walked in the garden
and sought out our parents even in their naked fear.
You never allow your people to be alone,
but stand close to us in the terrors of the night.
Jesus, your beloved, walked among us in our poverty,
embraced our fears,
and dispelled them in the glory of the Resurrection.
With the women martyrs of El Salvador,
and with your living witnesses,
Jesus continues to walk among us,
bringing the light of hope
where we are too often held in the darkness of oppression.

This night your Spirit moves among us once again
and beckons us deeper still to new deeds of justice and peace
until that final dawn,
when your truth and mercy shall bring to an end
all forms of despair and suffering.

Reading (from Elizabeth Johnson)
Wherever the gift of healing and liberation in however partial a
manner reaches the winterized or damaged earth, or peoples
crushed by war and injustice, or individual persons weary, harmed,
sick, or lost on life's journey, there the new creation in the Spirit is
happening.

Intercessions
God's heart always opens to the cries of the poor. Just as Jesus
walked among us to bring the mercy of God to the lowly, so too do we
offer our needs to God, as we pray: *Keep us mindful of your love.*

- For all Christians, that our baptism into the ministry of Christ
  may consecrate us daily for the service of the poor, let us pray...
- For every nation, that governments and leaders may make
  the peace of the Gospel the foundation of every constitution,
  let us pray...
- For all those whose life of justice and peace is a living
  martyrdom for the raising up of the poor and the enslaved,
  let us pray...
- For the downtrodden and those who are oppressed, that the
  spirit of God and the work of our hands may set them free,
  let us pray...

Closing Prayer
O God of justice, with Maura Clark, Ita Ford, Dorothy Kazel, and
Jean Donovan we celebrate the message of the Gospel that sets free

the captives of our world. Make us living witnesses to the freedom of Christ until that day when the blood of the martyrs will flower with the fullness of your peace. We ask this as all things through Jesus our Messiah forever and ever. Amen.

CHAPTER FIVE

"To Care for and Cultivate" (Genesis 1:26)

Prayers and Reflections on the Care of God's Creation

We Are Takers
Walter Brueggemann

You are the giver of all good things.
> All good things are sent from heaven above,
>> rain and sun,
>> day and night,
>> justice and righteousness,
>> bread to the eater and
>> seed to the sower,
>> peace to the old,
>> energy to the young,
>> joy to the babes.

We are takers, who take from you,
> day by day, daily bread,
> taking all we need as you supply,
> taking in gratitude and wonder and joy.

And then taking more,
> taking more than we need,
> taking more than you give us,
> taking from our sisters and brothers,
> taking from the poor and the weak,
>> taking because we are frightened, and so greedy,
>> taking because we are anxious, and so fearful,
>> taking because we are driven, and so uncaring.

Give us peace beyond our fear, and so end our greed.
Give us well-being beyond our anxiety, and so end our fear.
> Give us abundance beyond our drivenness, and so end our uncaring.

Turn our taking into giving...since we are in your giving image:
    Make us giving like you,
           giving gladly and not taking,
           giving in abundance, not taking,
           giving in joy, not taking,
           giving as he gave himself up for us all,
           giving, never taking. Amen.

A Prayer for Global Restoration
Michelle Balek, O.S.F.

Good and Gracious God,
Source of all Life,
all creation is charged with your Divine Energy.
Ignite your Spark within us,
that we may know ourselves
as truly human and holy,
irrevocably part of the Web of Life.
All creation
- each star and every flower,
- each drop of water and every person,
- each and every atom, down to its very electrons,
              explodes with the revelation
              of your Sacred Mystery.
Our minds alone cannot fathom such splendor.
Our hearts can only respond in awe, praise and gratitude.
Forgive us we pray, our ignorance
and insecurities which
- blind us to your Thumbprint writ large,
- deafen us to the sacred space
              between two heartbeats,
- prompt us in arrogance to demand and dominate,
- numb us to the destruction we've caused,
- hold us hostage to "either-or" thinking and living.
May we always walk gently upon this earth,
in right relationship,
- nurtured by your Love,
- taking only what we need,
- giving back to the earth in gratitude,
- sharing what we have,

- honoring all with reverence,
- reconciling and healing,
- mindful of those who will come after,
- recognizing our proper place as part of,
        not apart from, your creation.
Grant us the strength and courage, we pray,
for such radical transformation into your kin-dom.
Then we, too, with the very stones will shout,
"HOSANNA"

Note: "Kindom" denotes a world in which we recognize that we are related, that we are "kin" in God, and work to build relationships of love, peace and justice with all of creation.

Prayer at Harvest and Thanksgiving

O God, source and giver of all things,
you manifest your infinite majesty, power and goodness
in the earth about us;
we give you honor and glory.
For the sun and the rain,
for the manifold fruits of our fields;
for the increase of our herds and flocks,
we thank you.
For the enrichment of our souls with divine grace,
we are grateful.

Supreme Lord of the harvest,
graciously accept us and the fruits of our toil,
in union with Jesus, your Son,
as atonement for our sins,
for the growth of your Church,
for peace and love in our homes,
and for salvation for all.
We pray through Christ our Lord. Amen.

Prayer to Saint Clare

Saint Clare
whose name means light,
illumine our minds
with knowledge
and our hearts with love.

Enlarge our perceptions through the
inventiveness of God-given human
power. Give us an appreciation of
technology and the courage to channel
its wondrous energy to transform lives.

May we who are dedicated to your
name also imitate your steadfast faith
in serving our Creator forever.

We ask this through Jesus, our Brother.
Amen.

Prayer of Thanksgiving
Walter Rauschenbusch

O God, we thank you for this earth, our home;
for the wide sky and the blessed sun,
for the salt sea and the running water,
for the everlasting hills
and the never-resting winds,
for trees and the common grass underfoot.
We thank you for our senses
by which we hear the songs of birds,
and see the splendor of the summer fields,
and taste of the autumn fruits,
and rejoice in the feel of the snow,
and smell the breath of the spring.
Grant us a heart wide open to all this beauty;
and save our souls from being so blind
that we pass unseeing
when even the common thornbush
is aflame with your glory,
O God our creator,
who lives and reigns for ever and ever.

A Prayer of Saint Francis of Assisi

My little sisters the birds, you are much beholden to God your
Creator, and always and in every place you ought to praise Him. He
has given you double and triple gifts; He has given you freedom to go
into every place, and also preserved you in the ark of Noah, in order
that your kind might not perish from the earth. Again, you are
beholden to Him for the element of air which He has appointed for
you; moreover, you sow not, neither do you reap, and God feeds you
and gives you the rivers and the fountains for your drink; He gives
you the mountains and the valleys for your refuge, and the tall trees
wherein to build your nests, and as you can neither spin nor sew
God clothes you, you and your children. Your Creator loves you
much, since He has dealt so bounteously with you: and so beware,
little sisters of mine, of the sin of ingratitude, but ever strive to
praise God.

Canticle of the Creatures
Saint Francis of Assisi

Most high, almighty, good Lord!
All praise, glory, honor and exaltation are yours!
To you alone do they belong,
And no mere mortal dares pronounce your name.

Praise to you, O Lord our God, for all your creatures:
First, for our dear Brother Sun,
Who gives us the day
And illumines us with his light;
Fair is he, in splendor radiant,
Bearing your very likeness, O Lord.

For our Sister Moon,
And for the bright shining stars:
We praise you, O Lord.

For our Brother Wind,
For fair and stormy seasons
And all heaven's varied moods,
By which you nourish all that you have made:
We praise you, O Lord.

For our Sister Water,
So useful, lowly, precious and pure:
We praise you, O Lord.

For our Brother Fire,
Who brightens up our darkest nights:
Beautiful is he and eager,

Invincible and keen:
We praise you, O Lord.

For our Mother Earth,
Who sustains and feeds us,
Producing fair fruits, many colored flowers and herbs:
We praise you, O Lord.

For those who forgive one another for love of you,
And who patiently bear sickness and other trials.
Happy are they who peacefully endure;
You will crown them, O Most High!
We praise you, O Lord.

All creatures,
Praise and glorify my Lord
And give him thanks
And serve him in great humility.
We praise you, O Lord.

A Penitential Litany
United States Conference of Catholic Bishops

Leader: Lord God, your peace demands justice for all and calls us to transform ourselves, our communities, our nation, and our world.
Response: Lord, have mercy.

Leader: We confess, O Lord, as creatures privileged with the care and keeping of your creation, that we have abused your gifts of creation through arrogance, ignorance and greed.
Response: Lord, have mercy.

Leader: We confess, O Lord, that we have risked permanent damage to your handiwork; we confess impoverishing creation's ability to bring you praise.
Response: Lord, have mercy.

Leader: We confess, O Lord, that the races and cultures of the earth reflect the richness of your creation and that we have too often mistreated and inflicted injustices upon the poor, minorities, and the marginalized.
Response: Lord, have mercy.

Leader: O Lord, how long will it take before we awaken to what we have done? How many waters must we pollute? How many forests must we destroy? How much soil must we erode and poison, O Lord? How long will we deny the cries of the poor?
Response: Lord, have mercy.

Leader: How much of the earth's atmosphere must we contaminate? How many species must we abuse and extinguish? How many people must we degrade and kill with toxic wastes before we learn to love and respect your creation and our sisters and brothers? Before we learn to love and respect our fragile planet home?

Response: For our sins and failings, O God, we ask forgiveness.

Leader: In sorrow for what we have done, we repent. We ask you, O Lord, to forgive our sins and send your Spirit to renew us and the face of the earth. Grant this through Christ our Lord.

Response: Amen.

U.N. Environmental Sabbath Prayer

Great Spirit,
give us hearts to understand;
never to take
from creation's beauty more than we give,
never to destroy wantonly for the furtherance of
greed;
never to deny to give our hands for the building of
earth's beauty;
never to take from her what we cannot use.
Give us hearts to understand that to destroy the earth's
music is to create confusion;
that to wreck her appearance is to blind us to beauty;
that to callously pollute her fragrance is to make a
house of stench;
that as we care for her she will care for us. Amen.

CHAPTER SIX

"Guide Our Feet Into the Way of Peace" (Luke 1:79)

Prayers and Reflections on Peace

Lead Me to Peace
Satish Kumar

Lead me from death to life,
from falsehood to truth.
Lead me from despair to hope,
from fear to trust.
Lead me from hate to love,
from war to peace.
Let peace fill our hearts,
our world, our universe,
Peace, Peace, Peace.

Peace Prayer
Attributed to Saint Francis of Assisi

Lord, make us instruments of your peace.
Where there is hatred, let us sow love;
where there is injury, pardon;
where there is doubt, faith;
where there is despair, hope;
where there is darkness, light;
and where there is sadness, joy.

O Divine Master, grant that we may not
so much seek to be consoled as to console;
to be understood as to understand;
to be loved as to love;
for it is in giving that we receive;
it is in pardoning that we are pardoned;
and it is in dying that we are born to eternal life.

Peace for the Children of God
Archbishop Desmond M. Tutu

O God, all holy one,
you are our Mother and our Father,
and we are your children.
Open our eyes and our hearts
so that we may be able to discern
your work in the universe.
And be able to see Your features
in every one of Your children.
May we learn that there are many paths
but all lead to You.
Help us to know that you have created us
for family, for togetherness,
for peace, for gentleness,
for compassion, for caring, for sharing.

May we know that You want us
to care for one another
as those who know
that they are sisters and brothers,
members of the same family,
Your family,
the human family.

Help us to beat our swords into plowshares
and our spears into pruning hooks,
so that we may be able to live
in peace and harmony,
wiping away the tears
from the eyes of those

who are less fortunate than ourselves.
And may we know war no more,
as we strive to be
what You want us to be:
Your children.
Amen.

Evangelization
Archbishop Oscar Romero

A Christian community is evangelized in order to evangelize.
A light is lit in order to give light.
A candle is not lit to be put under a bushel, said Christ.
It is lit and put up high in order to give light.

That is what a true community is like.
A community is a group of men and women who have found the
truth in Christ and in His Gospel, and who follow the truth and join
together to follow it more strongly.

It is not just an individual conversion but a community conversion.
It is a family that believes, a group that accepts God.

In the group, each one finds that the brother or sister is a source of
strength and that in moments of weakness they help one another,
and by loving one another and believing, they give light.

The preacher no longer needs to preach, for there are Christians
who preach by their own lives.

I said once and I repeat today that if, unhappily, some day they
silence our radio and don't let us write our newspaper, each of you
who believe must become a microphone, a radio station, a
loudspeaker, not to talk but to call for faith.

I am not afraid that our faith may depend only on the archbishop's
preaching. I don't think that I'm that important.

I believe that this message, which is only a humble echo of God's
word, enters our hearts, not because it is mine, but because it comes
from God.

Prayer for the Destruction of the Enemy
Mark Twain

O Lord our Father, our young patriots, idols of our hearts, go forth to battle—be Thou near them! With them—in spirit—we also go forth from the sweet peace of our beloved firesides to smite the foe. O Lord our God, help us to tear their soldiers to bloody shreds with our shells; help us to cover their smiling fields with the pale forms of their patriot dead; help us to drown the thunder of the guns with the shrieks of their wounded, writhing in pain; help us to lay waste their humble homes with a hurricane of fire; help us to wring the hearts of their unoffending widows with unavailing grief; help us to turn them out roofless with their little children to wander unfriended the wastes of their desolated land in rags and hunger and thirst, sports of the sun flames of summer and the icy winds of winter, broken in spirit, worn with travail, imploring Thee for the refuge of the grave and denied it—for our sakes who adore Thee, Lord, blast their hopes, blight their lives, protract their bitter pilgrimage, make heavy their steps, water their way with their tears, stain the white snow with the blood of their wounded feet! We ask it, in the spirit of love, of Him who is the Source of Love, and who is the ever-faithful refuge and friend of all that are sore beset and seek His aid with humble and contrite hearts. Amen.

Note: Satirist Mark Twain wrote "The War Prayer" (from which this is taken) to illustrate that every prayer for success in battle carries with it a second, unuttered prayer for the destruction of the enemy.

Hands of Mary

Caryll Houselander

The circle of a girl's arms has changed the world, the round, sorrowful world, to a cradle for God. O Mother of God, be hands that are rocking the world to a kind of rhythm of love; that the incoherence of war and the chaos of unrest be soothed to a lullaby, and the round, sorrowful world, in your hands, the cradle of God.

Their Plowshares Are Beat Into Swords
Walter Brueggemann

And now their plowshares are beat into swords—as are ours.
  now their pruning hooks are beat into spears—as are ours.
    Not only swords and spears,
      but bullets, and bombs, and missiles,
        of steel on flesh,
          of power against bodies...
And you, in your indignation sound your mantra,
  "Blessed are the peacemakers."
  We dare to believe they are the aggressor,
        and we are the peacemaker.
  Yet in sober night dream, we glance otherwise
        and think we may be aggressor,
        as we vision rubbled homes,
          murdered civilians,
          and charred babies.
And you, in our sadness, sound your mantra,
  "Blessed are the peacemakers."
  We do not love war,
  we yearn for peace,
      but we have lost much will for peace
      even while we dream of order.
And you, in your hope, sound your mantra,
  "Blessed are the peacemakers."
  Deliver us from excessive certitude about ourselves.
  Hold us in the deep ambiguity where we find ourselves,
  Show us yet again the gaping space
          between your will and our feeble
    imagination.

Sound your mantra with more authority,
> with more indignation,
> through sadness,
> in hope... "Blessed are the peacemakers."
Only peacemakers are blessed.
> We find ourselves well short of blessed.
> Give us freedom for your deep otherwise,
> finally to be blessed,
> in the name of the Peacemaker
> who gave and did not take. Amen.

Prayer for World Peace
Joan D. Chittister, O.S.B.

Great God, who has told us
"Vengeance is mine,"
save us from ourselves,
save us from the vengeance in our hearts
and the acid in our souls.

Save us from our desire to hurt as we have been hurt,
to punish as we have been punished,
to terrorize as we have been terrorized.

Give us the strength it takes
to listen rather than to judge,
to trust rather than to fear,
to try again and again
to make peace even when peace eludes us.

We ask, O God, for the grace
to be our best selves.
We ask for the vision
to be builders of the human community
rather than its destroyers.
We ask for the humility as a people
to understand the fears and hopes of other peoples.
We ask for the love it takes
to bequeath to the children of the world to come
more than the failures of our own making.
We ask for the heart it takes
to care for all the peoples
of Afghanistan and Iraq, of Palestine and Israel
as well as for ourselves.

Give us the depth of soul, O God,
to constrain our might,
to resist the temptations of power,
to refuse to attack the attackable,
to understand
that vengeance begets violence,
and to bring peace—not war—wherever we go.

For You, O God, have been merciful to us.
For You, O God, have been patient with us.
For You, O God, have been gracious to us.

And so may we be merciful
and patient
and gracious
and trusting
with these others whom you also love.

This we ask through Jesus,
the one without vengeance in his heart.
This we ask forever and ever. Amen.

Prayer for Peace
Pope John Paul II
Hiroshima, February 25, 1981

To the Creator
  of nature and humanity,
  of truth and beauty, I pray:

Hear my voice, for it is the voice of the victims
  of all wars and violence among individuals and nations.

Hear my voice, for it is the voice of all children
  who suffer and will suffer when people put their faith
  in weapons and war.

Hear my voice when I beg you to instill into the hearts
  of all human beings the wisdom of peace,
  the strength of justice and the joy of fellowship.

Hear my voice, for I speak for the multitudes
  in every country and every period of history
  who do not want war and
  are ready to walk the road of peace.

Hear my voice, and grant insight and strength
  so that we may always respond to hatred with love,
  to injustice with total dedication to justice,
  to need with sharing of self, to war with peace.

O God, hear my voice, and grant unto the world
  Your everlasting peace.

Prayer of Nonviolence
John Dear, S.J.

God of Nonviolence,
Thank you for the gift of your love and your peace.
Give me the grace to live the life of Gospel nonviolence
that I might be a faithful follower of the nonviolent Jesus.

Send the Holy Spirit of nonviolence upon me that I will love everyone,
from my neighbor to my enemies,
that I may see you in everyone, and know everyone as my sister and brother,
and never hurt or fear anyone again.

Make me an instrument of your peace,
that I might give my life in the struggle for justice and disarmament;
that I may work for the abolition of war, poverty and nuclear weapons;
that I may always respond with love and never retaliate with violence;
that I may accept suffering in the struggle of justice and never inflict suffering or death on others;
that I my live more simply, in solidarity with the world's poor,
that I may defend the poor and resist systemic injustice and institutionalized violence,
that I may always choose life and resist the forces of death.

Guide me on the Way of nonviolence.
Help me to speak the truth of peace, to practice boundless compassion, to radiate unconditional love, to forgive everyone who ever hurt me, to embody your nonviolence, to walk with you in contemplative peace, to be your beloved servant and friend.

Disarm my heart, and I shall be your instrument to disarm other hearts and the world. Lead me, God of nonviolence, with the whole human family, into your nonviolent reign of justice and peace where there is no more war, no more injustice, no more poverty, no more nuclear weapons, no more violence.

I ask this in the name of the nonviolent Jesus, our brother and our peace. Amen.

Not Now
Marianne Hieb, R.S.M.

Don't let us go to war now
When the field has just been planted
When the poem's half-begun
When the rich beef stew has found the fire
When the child-seed bursts to life-form
When his fledgling play is ripe for stage
When the song is near-recorded
When the dance is almost learned
When the swing-set is at last put up
In green back-yards where children run
When horizons meet our oceans
When full eyes can meet dear faces
When the dreaming comes.

Don't let us go to war now
When youth is on the brink of shining
When orchids can be grown at home
When prism facets break the colors brilliantly
Don't let us go to war.

Don't let us fight ourselves now
Don't give us cause to wail now
Don't listen to our screechings that are searing other lands
Reach the screechings.
Burst the prismed places of our unknowing groanings
Into human colors
That will take our breath away
By beauty
Not by death.

Give us back our breathing
For the dancing
And the song
For the swing-set
And the youth
And for all horizons, far and near
Here and there.

While the growing orchids grace us
And the fields are firm with seedlings
And we are finished poems,
Feeding on the taste of readied stew
And savoring our stock again
This fleeting human stock.

Pray for Peace
Ellen Bass

Pray to whomever you kneel down to:
Jesus nailed to his wooden or plastic cross,
his suffering face bent to kiss you,
Buddha still under the Bo tree in scorching heat,
Adonai, Allah. Raise your arms to Mary
that she may lay her palm on our brows,
to Shekhina, Queen of Heaven and Earth,
to Inanna in her stripped descent.

Hawk or Wolf, or the Great Whale, the Record Keeper
of time before, time now, time ahead, pray. Bow down
to terriers and shepherds and Siamese cats.
Fields of artichokes and elegant strawberries.

Pray to the bus driver who takes you to work,
pray on the bus, for everyone riding that bus,
and for everyone riding buses all over the world.
If you haven't been on a bus in a long time,
climb the few steps, drop some silver, and pray.

Waiting in line for the movies, for the ATM,
for your latte and croissant, offer your plea.
Make your eating and drinking a supplication.
Make your slicing of carrots a holy act,
each translucent layer of the onion, a deeper prayer.

Make the brushing of your hair
a prayer, every strand its own voice,
singing in the choir on your head.
As you wash your face, the water slipping

through your fingers, a prayer: water,
softest thing on earth, gentleness
that wears away rock.

Making love, of course, is already prayer.
Skin, and open mouths worshiping that skin,
the fragile case we are poured into,
each caress a season of peace.

If you're hungry, pray. If you're tired.
Pray to Gandhi and Dorothy Day.
Shakespeare. Sappho. Sojourner Truth.
Pray to the angels and the ghost of your grandfather.

When you walk to your car, to the mailbox,
to the video store, let each step
be a prayer that we all keep our legs,
that we do not blow off anyone else's legs.
Or crush their skulls.
And if you are riding on a bicycle
or a skateboard, in a wheelchair, each revolution
of the wheels a prayer that as the earth revolves
we will do *less harm, less harm, less harm.*

And as you work, typing with a new manicure,
a tiny palm tree painted on one pearlescent nail
or delivering soda, or drawing good blood
into rubber-capped vials, writing on a blackboard
with yellow chalk, twirling pizzas, pray for peace.

With each breath in, take in the faith of those
who have believed when belief seemed foolish,

who persevered. With each breath out, cherish.
Pull weeds for peace, turn over in your sleep for peace,
feed the birds, each shiny seed
that spills onto the earth, another second of peace.
Wash your dishes, call your mother, drink wine.

Shovel leaves or snow or trash from your sidewalk.
Make a path. Fold a photo of a dead child
around your VISA card. Gnaw your crust
of prayer, scoop your prayer water from the gutter.
Mumble along like a crazy person, stumbling
your prayer through the streets.

Student's Prayer for Peace

I need reminders of my inner worth,
reminders stronger than my doubts,
deeper than the compliments of friends,
more lasting than discouragement or fear.
Help me to learn your inner way of peace.

Show me the preciousness of every life:
the poor whose dignity is wrapped in rags,
the weak who carry toughness as a shield,
the frightened pretending they are brave.
Help me to learn your gentle way of peace.

Make me aware of other people's pain,
whether from sickness, guns, or words.
Let me be touched by their afflicted lives
and make my life more generous and fair.
Help me to learn your healing way of peace.

Open my mind to see opposing truths
teach me to listen to all who disagree,
honoring their values and their voice,
stretching my vision to include another view.
Help me to learn your loving way of peace.

Give me patience and the time to grow:
time to practice what I know you teach;
patience for the seeds of peace to sprout,
to blossom and bear fruit for all my life.
Help me to learn your patient way of peace.

Litany of Mary of Nazareth

Glory to you, God our Creator...
Breathe into us new life, new meaning.
Glory to you, God our Savior...
Lead us in the way of peace and justice.
Glory to you, healing Spirit...
Transform us to empower others.

Mary, wellspring of peace...*Be our guide.*
Model of strength
Model of gentleness
Model of trust
Model of courage
Model of patience
Model of risk
Model of openness
Model of perseverance

Mother of the liberator... *Pray for us.*
Mother of the homeless
Mother of the dying
Mother of the nonviolent
Widowed mother
Unwed mother
Mother of a political prisoner
Mother of the condemned
Mother of the executed criminal

Oppressed woman... *Lead us to life.*
Liberator of the oppressed
Marginalized woman
Comforter of the afflicted

Cause of our joy
Sign of contradiction
Breaker of bondage
Political refugee
Seeker of sanctuary
First disciple
Sharer in Christ's passion
Seeker of God's will
Witness to Christ's resurrection

Woman of mercy...*Empower us.*
Woman of faith
Woman of contemplation
Woman of vision
Woman of wisdom and understanding
Woman of grace and truth
Woman, pregnant with hope
Woman, centered in God

Mary, Queen of Peace,
> we entrust our lives to you.
> Shelter us from war, hatred and oppression.

Teach us
> to live in peace,
> to educate ourselves for peace.
Inspire us to act justly,
> to revere all God has made.
Root peace firmly in our hearts
> and in our world.

Amen.

The Prayer of Saint Francis, Updated
John Dear, S.J.

Lord make me an instrument of your peace—
Let me serve as a channel of your love and peace, a reconciler of
peoples, an apostle of Gospel nonviolence. Help me to love all
people, including the enemies of my country. Use me as a voice and
instrument for nuclear and total disarmament. Make me a witness to
your way of suffering love and redemptive goodwill. Use me in your
struggle to liberate the oppressed, create justice for the poor, resist
systemic injustice, topple the idols of death, denounce the gods of
war, and beat swords into plowshares. Use me to unmask the false
peace of the world, which buries the cry of the poor, the blood of the
oppressed, the victims of war. Use me to create your peace, the
peace which comes through the nonviolent cross and resurrection.
Fashion me into a person of contemplative nonviolence; a person of
prayer, mindfulness, harmony, and wisdom. Let me radiate your
disarming grace and light and presence to all.

Where there is hatred, let me sow love—
Transform the hatred in my own heart into your love,
understanding, compassion, forgiveness and grace. Disarm me so
that hatred disappears and love flows freely. Use me to build bridges
between divided peoples, to soothe their fears, to see one another as
sisters and brothers. Let me sow the seeds of love that will bear fruit
in a new spirit of repentance, mercy, disarmament, justice and
liberation for the poor. Extinguish the flames of war and spring
forth your life-giving waters of love—in the church, between the
races and the genders, the rich and the poor, the old and the young,
in Baghdad and Washington, D.C., in Calcutta and Mississippi, in
Rwanda and East Timor, in Haiti and El Salvador, in South Africa
and the Philippines, between East and West, North and South. Help

me to sow seeds of agape, compassion and peace, and to water and care for those seeds that they may flower into your reign of nonviolence.

Where there is injury, let me sow pardon—
That I may forgive seventy times seven times, and teach forgiveness by my life; vowing like the Buddha compassion toward all living things for the rest of my life; healing especially those who have lost loved ones to violence and murder, that they may forgive those who murdered their loved ones. May we as a people grant clemency to all, including those who have murdered. May the death penalty be abolished, deterrence discarded, and the just war theory thrown away. May healing, repentance and forgiveness be the new spirit of the times. May we repent for our use of nuclear weapons on the people of Hiroshima and Nagasaki and apologize; may we pardon all crimes of war and genocide by disarming our arsenal to ensure that they never happen again. May all claim their true identity as your children; and may you continue to forgive us our sins, our rejection of you, and our violence to you on the cross.

Where there is doubt, faith in you—
In the midst of this culture of death—faithless, insecure, fearful, idolatrous, vengeful, arrogant, materialistic; in the doubting church, believing in the culture's empty promises, illusions, material goods, idols of death, the false security of its bombs and militarism instead of you; let me sow seeds of living faith in You. Help us to trust you who remain faithful to us. Let our faith manifest itself in the committed lives we live, true to the Gospel, to your way of nonviolence and suffering love. Let us keep your covenant of peace and remain faithful to you yourself, our gentle father, our loving mother, our faithful God.

Where there is despair, only hope—
Low grade despair and high octane desperation; no win situations
with no way out; in the midst of anxiety, panic, loneliness, fear,
devastation, poverty, war, death itself—there, let me sow hope, the
seeds of resurrection, a way out of no way; new possibilities, new
life, the life that overcomes death; the seeds of reconciliation, love,
and confident trust in God. Let me instill the gift of peace, the dawn
of a new day, the promise of resurrection, the vision of the promised
land where there is no more war, no more nuclear weapons, no
more violence, no more injustice, no more poverty, no more misery,
no more fear—only love and you, the God of resurrection, standing
warmly in our midst.

Where there is darkness, light—
Amidst the darkness in our hearts, the sin of violence, our self-
hatred, our fear, our hostility toward one another, our oppression of
the poor, our rejection of you; let your light shine—the light of
peace, joy, love, trust; the light of truth, the light of resurrection, the
light of hope. Let us be like Christ, the light of the world, pointing to
your presence, showing each other how to live justly, humanly,
nonviolently, and compassionately. Let us burn with love, truth,
faith, peace and justice, so that our light, your light, will shine for all
and one day, we see you face to face.

Where there is sorrow, joy—
In this world of sorrow and grief, desolation and depression,
sadness and death, in hearts dulled from hostility and hatred,
deadened by the bomb's shadow, by the despair of imperial
oppression, the race for money, the loss of love and loved ones; in
the hearts grown cold by horror upon horror, a nuclear blast upon
the human spirit—there, put in us the joy of your resurrection, your
joy now complete, the dawn of that new morning, when you stand by

the shore, alive, welcoming, forgiving. Let us taste the joy of shalom which the world can never take away from us.

O Divine Master—
Jesus; God of Life; Human One; Compassionate, Nonviolent Savior; Prince of Peace; Mercy within Mercy within Mercy; Resister of Evil; the Way, the Truth, and the Life; Good Shepherd; our Beloved, our Brother, our Bread, our Breath—

Grant that I may seek not so much to be consoled as to console—
Not to be the center of attention, to strive for praise and honor, to let my domineering ego, proud and arrogant, run rampant; instead, may I comfort others, bring them peace and warmth, safety and affection, unconditional love and kindness, and not cause anyone to be afraid in my presence, but to be at ease, at peace, relaxed, content because it is not so much me they see, but your presence shining transparently through me. May I speak the truth, denounce injustice, proclaim the good news of your justice, your jubilee year, the liberation of all from violence and death, and as I invite people to the way of the cross, and undergo it myself, may others be consoled in the hope, joy, and confidence of your resurrection, in your coming reign of peace at hand here and now.

To be understood, as to understand—
May I not be focused on argument, anger, fury, resentment, self-righteousness, indignation, or arrogance, but rather, let me understand every one else, listen to their pain, feel their sorrow, know their burdens, share their hopes and joys, weep when they weep and rejoice when they rejoice, be attentive to their needs and always, put others first. Let me know every human being as my sister and brother.

To be loved, as to love—
Grant that I may not so much seek selfishly the love of others,
insisting on my rights and needs, but instead, to love others
selflessly, generously, beyond measure, unconditionally, without
any desire for reciprocation, without any expectation of service in
return; a love that is willing to suffer for others; that will lay down
my life for others in the nonviolent struggle for peace, for justice for
the poor, for protection of the earth and all living things; a love even
for my enemies, my persecutors; a love that insists on truth, that
resists evil nonviolently, that reflects your own love for all people, a
love that radiates your love present in my own spirit calling me your
beloved.

For it is in giving that we receive—
By giving selflessly, sacrificially all that we have, as you did for us
dying on the cross in the struggle for justice and truth; by sharing
our resources with the poor, sharing our lives with one another,
sharing our faith, hope and love with all people—we receive a
hundred times more—life, love, friends, faith, hope, peace, and joy.
We receive your blessing, your wisdom, your mercy, your love, your
presence, You yourself.

It is in pardoning that we are pardoned—
That I may forgive everyone who has ever hurt me, especially those
closest to me, my family, my friends, my community; that I may let
go of all resentment, grudges, anger, bitterness and hostility; that I
may see only your love, present in everyone; concentrate on your
abiding presence, and so love all; that I may grant clemency to all
and so win clemency for myself and all; that I may pardon others as
you have already pardoned me and continue to pardon me; that I
may resist war, injustice and poverty through the steadfast
nonviolent resistance that risks my life yet already forgives all who

persecute me, so that your reign of forgiveness and compassion may be proclaimed.

It is in dying that we are born to eternal life.
Through our own deaths, the peaceful letting go of our lives, everyday of our lives, until our final breath, may we experience life and go deeper into new life; by entering your paschal mystery, by sharing in your cross—the way of nonviolent resistance to systemic injustice, the way of compassion and truth, justice and love, the way of redemptive love through unearned suffering, willingly accepted without even the desire for retaliation. By sharing in your death, Jesus, we are born into the new life of your resurrection and enter into the paradise of your peace to live with you, the saints, and the God of life, in perfect joy, forever and ever.

Amen. *Alleluia.*

CHAPTER SEVEN

"It Is Enough for the Disciple to Be Like the Teacher" (Matthew 10:25)

Prayers and Reflections on Discipleship

Prophets of a Future Not Our Own
Bishop Kenneth Untener

It helps, now and then, to step back and take the long view.
The kingdom is not only beyond our efforts; it is even beyond our vision.

We accomplish in our lifetime only a tiny fraction of the magnificent enterprise that is God's work.
Nothing we do is complete, which is another way of saying that the kingdom always lies beyond us.
No statement says all that could be said. No prayer fully expresses our faith.
No confession brings perfection, no pastoral visit brings wholeness.
No program accomplishes totally the church's mission.
No set of goals and objectives includes everything.

This is what we are all about. We plant the seeds that one day will grow.
We water seeds already planted, knowing that they hold future promise.
We lay foundations that will need further development. We provide yeast that produces effects far beyond our capabilities.

We cannot do everything, and there is a sense of liberation in realizing that. This enables us to do something, and to do it very well.
It may be incomplete, but it is a beginning, a step along the way, an opportunity for the Lord's grace to enter and do the rest.

We may never see the end results, but that is the difference between the master builder and the worker.

We are workers, not master builders, ministers, not messiahs.
We are prophets of a future not our own. Amen.

A Prayer for Public Discipleship
Reverend Richard Fragomeni

How holy and wonderful are you, O God of Mercy and Justice. From
the beginning, your excessive love created the universe and
fashioned us in your own image and likeness. When sin scarred the
beauty of your handiwork and ingratitude weakened the pulse of
history, you did not give up on us. Rather, in Jesus of Nazareth, you
worked the marvel of a new creation, giving us life in abundance.

In an outpouring of service, Jesus entered into the chaos of pain and
suffering and became the first disciple of his own discipleship. He
emptied himself as the servant of creation and boldly proclaimed to
all who would receive him, a more humane and graceful culture and
society. His death and resurrection promised a future to his
mission.

Your incredible energy of creation is still active among us in the
Holy Spirit, whom Jesus left as a gift to hungry hearts. In this Spirit,
you have inspired us to publicly illustrate our commitment to the
work of Christ's mission. In this Spirit, we are honored to be called
his disciples, extending your creative love to the end of time.

May we be worthy of being your ambassadors of life to others,
sharing the discipleship of Christ as our greatest praise, and serving
the works of justice and mercy as our greatest thanks.

Amen.

Peace to You
Cardinal John Newman

God has created me to do Him some definite service;
He has committed some work to me which He has not
committed to another. I have my mission—I may never
know it in this life, but I shall be told it in the next.

I am a link in a chain, a bond of connection between
persons. He has not created me for nothing.
I shall do good. I shall do His work. I shall be an angel of
peace, a preacher of truth in my own place while not
intending it—if I do but keep His Commandments.

Therefore, I will trust Him. Whatever, wherever I am
I can never be thrown away.
If I am in sickness, my sickness may serve Him;
in perplexity, my perplexity may serve Him;
If I am in sorrow, my sorrow may serve Him.
He does nothing in vain.
He knows what He is about.
He may take away my friends.
He may throw me among strangers.
He may make me feel desolate, make my spirits sink,
hide my future from me—still He knows what He is about.

Give Us Courage
Karl Rahner

Holy Creator of the universe, of the earth and its people, you have allowed humanity to run astray in wholesale madness throughout history, wherefore nothing remains for us but to sink to our knees in tears before you who created us. Give us all the courage and valor to achieve peace and real disarmament. Give the Church the courage to teach not how one can cleverly reconcile the egotism among us, but rather how in light of the folly of the cross one can, and indeed must, assume direct responsibility for unconditional justice and peace. Convert the hearts of the mighty so that they may not yield to the deceitful pursuit of power in order to justify their own actions, nor deceive themselves and others while claiming to serve the ends of peace by proliferating arms. And ultimately: teach us within our own lives to further the cause of peace unselfishly.

Christ Has No Body
Attributed to Saint Teresa of Avila

Christ has no body now but yours,
No hands but yours,
No feet but yours.

Yours are the eyes through which
Christ's compassion must look out on the world.

Yours are the feet with which
He is to go about doing good.

Yours are the hands with which
He is to bless us now.

Not Enough
Monsignor Geno C. Baroni

Lord, I pray: Help me to know that our limited charity is not enough.
Lord, help me to know that our soup kitchens and secondhand
clothes are not enough. Lord, help me to know it is not enough for
the Church to be the ambulance service that goes around picking up
the broken pieces of humanity for American society. Lord, help us
all to know that God's judgment demands justice from us as a rich
and powerful nation.

Let us pray that the Holy Spirit will provide new gifts to meet new
needs. Let us pray that there will be new voices of justice, new
prophets who will hear the words of the Lord and stand up, as
Christians, to say: Yes, the Spirit of the Lord is upon me. He has sent
me to bring glad tidings to the poor.

Prayer for Educators of Justice and Peace
Jane Deren

Good and Gracious God, Teacher of all peoples, Bless and guide those of us who seek to educate others about your good news of justice and peace.

Guide us in our work, as we reach out to shape hearts and minds.

Walk with us as we deal with complex issues, help us to find the right words and actions to communicate your love for all members of the global family.

Support us as we promote critical reflections on local, national and international issues. Renew our commitment, so we can spark courage and empower others to confront injustice.

Allow our vision of a better world to transform spirits. Help us to nurture the skills that will bring this vision to reality.

Remind us how blessed we are to have this call to proclaim justice and peace and to be able to respond even in small ways.

Give us patience and perseverance in our work. Grace us with fellowship and community. Help us to remember that you are our rest and refreshment. Amen.

Prayer for Peace and Justice
United States Conference of Catholic Bishops

God, source of all light,
we are surrounded by the darkness of
the injustices experienced by your people,
the poor who are hungry and who search
for shelter, the sick who seek relief,
and the downtrodden who seek help
in their hopelessness.

Surround us and fill us with your Spirit who is Light.
Lead us in your way to be light to your people.
Help our parish to be salt for our community
as we share your love with those caught
in the struggles of life.

We desire to be your presence to the least among us
and to know your presence in them as we work through you
to bring justice and peace to this world in desperate need.

We ask this through our Lord Jesus Christ,
your Son, who lives and reigns with you
and the Holy Spirit, one God, for ever and ever. Amen.

We Notice Your Giving
Walter Brueggemann

You God of command who issues demands upon us;
You God of promise who compels us to hope;
You God of deliverance endlessly up-ending our systems of abuse;
In all your commanding, your promising, your delivering,
        we notice your *giving*.
            Indeed your giving is what we notice first, best, and most,
                about your own life...
            giving without reserve or limitation.
You give us worlds of beauty and abundance,
            blessed and fruitful,
You give us sustenance for the day,
                so that we are not smitten by the sun by day
                    or by the moon by night.
You give us—in the center of all your giving—
            your only, well-beloved Son.
You give us your spirit of power, energy, and wisdom.
            gifts all without grudging!
And we receive, because we have no alternative,
            because we cannot live without your gifts,
            because we have nothing but what you have
                given us.
We receive, carefully and anxiously,
            worried that there is not enough,
                of security and safety,
                of grades or grants or dollars or friends,
                of sex or beer or SUVs,
                    or students and endowments,
                of futures, and so we crave and store up
                    for rainy futures.

We receive occasionally when you stagger us
    and we break beyond anxiety,
        in gratitude,
            recognizing that you in your generosity
                give us more than enough,
            and in grateful giving we become our true selves,
                breathed in the image of your Son.
So we ponder your generosity and are dazzled.
We measure our gratitude and our capacity to be generous.
    We pray your haunting us beyond ourselves,
        in wonder at your way,
        in love for the world you love,
        in praise that transforms our fear,
        in wonder, love and praise,
            or lives beyond ourselves,
                toward us,
                a blessing in the world.
Hear us as we pray in the name of the emptied, exalted One. Amen.

Make Us Uncomfortable
Archbishop Dom Helder Camara

Come Lord
Do not smile and say
you are already with us.
Millions do not know you
and to us who do,
What is the difference?
What is the point of your presence
if our lives do not alter?
Change our lives,
shatter our complacency.
Make your word
flesh of our flesh,
blood of our blood
and our life's purpose.
Take away the quietness
of a clear conscience.
Press us uncomfortably.
For only thus is
that other peace made,
your peace.

From *Thoughts in Solitude*
Thomas Merton

My Lord God, I have no idea where I am going. I do not see the road ahead of me. I cannot know for certain where it will end. Nor do I really know myself, and the fact that I think that I am following your will does not mean that I am actually doing so. But I believe that the desire to please you does in fact please you. And I hope I have that desire in all that I am doing. I hope that I will never do anything apart from that desire. And I know that if I do this you will lead me by the right road, though I may know nothing about it. Therefore I will trust you always though I may seem to be lost and in the shadow of death. I will not fear, for you are ever with me, and you will never leave me to face my perils alone.

Affirmation of Faith Hispanic Creed
Justo L. Gonzalez

We believe in God, the Father Almighty
Creator of the heavens and the earth;
Creator of all peoples and all cultures;
Creator of all tongues and all races.

We believe in Jesus Christ, God's son, our Lord,
God made flesh in a person for all humanity,
God made flesh in an age for all ages,
God made flesh in one culture for all cultures,
God made flesh in love and grace for all creation.

We believe in the Holy Spirit
through whom God incarnate in Jesus Christ
makes his presence known in our peoples and our cultures;
through whom, God, Creator of all that exists,
gives us power to become new creatures;
whose infinite gifts make us one people, the Body of Christ.

We believe in the Church Universal
because it is a sign of God's reign
whose faithfulness is shown in its many hues
where all the colors paint a single landscape,
where all tongues sing the same praise.

We believe in the reign of God—the day of the Great Fiesta
when all creation's colors will form a harmonious rainbow,
when all peoples will join in joyful banquet
when all tongues of the universe will sing the same song.

And, because we believe, we commit ourselves:
to believe for those who do not believe,
to love for those who do not love,
to dream for those who do not dream
until the day when hope becomes a reality. Amen.

Seeking Wisdom and Discernment
Thomas à Kempis

Grant me, O Lord,
to know what is worth knowing,
to love what is worth loving,
to praise what delights you most,
to value what is precious in your sight,
to hate what is offensive to you.
Do not let me judge by what I see,
nor pass sentence according to what I hear,
but to judge rightly between things that differ,
and above all to search out
and to do what pleases you,
through Jesus Christ our Lord.

Spirit of God
Huub Oosterhuis

We worship you, Holy Spirit of God,
and we may only guess, as best we can,
who you are for us.
We call you by human names and words
so that we need not be entirely silent.
We open up our hearts to receive you
That we may learn how deeply
and invisibly you are present everywhere.
You are the air we breathe,
the distance we gaze into,
the space that surrounds us...
We pray to you, Spirit of God, creator,
complete the work you have begun,
prevent the evil we are capable of doing
and inspire us toward what is good.

Christ's Table
Brian Wren and Betsy King

What do you bring to Christ's table?
We bring bread, made by many people's work,
from an unjust world
where some have plenty
and most go hungry.

At this table all are fed,
and no one turned away.
Thanks be to God.

What do you bring to Christ's table?
We bring wine,
made by many people's work,
from an unjust world
where some have leisure
and most struggle to survive.

At this table all share the cup
of pain and celebration,
and no one is denied.
Thanks be to God.

These gifts shall be for us
the body and blood of Christ.
Our witness against hunger,
our cry against injustice,
and our hope for a world
where God is fully known
and every child is fed.
Thanks be to God.

Harvest Us
Gabe Huck

What tears you cry, sower God, over us all.
But how you laugh in amazement
and what songs you sing
when there is some harvest.
Your saints from Adam and Eve,
from Moses and Miriam,
until our own grandparents and parents,
and we too,
need your tears
and long to hear your laughter.
Harvest us home to sing your praise
for ever and ever. Amen.

Tender God
Gabe Huck

Tender God,
seldom heard but ever persisting,
your word warns the powerful,
all of us whose choices this day
will bind and limit others.
Give us clear sight to know our sins
and tears to weep for such a world.

Prayer of the Iona Community in Scotland

You keep us waiting.
You, the God of all time,
       want us to wait for the right time in which to discover
       who we are, where we must go,
       who will be with us, and what we must do.
So, thank you...for the waiting time.

You keep us looking.
You, the God of all space,
       want us to look in the right and wrong places for signs of
       hope,
       for people who are hopeless,
       for visions of a better world that will appear among the
       disappointments of the world we know.
So, thank you...for the looking time.

You keep us loving.
You, the God whose name is love,
       want us to be like you—
       to love the loveless and the unlovely and the unlovable;
       to love without jealousy or design or threat,
       and most difficult of all, to love ourselves.
So, thank you...for the loving time.

And in all this you keep us,
       through hard questions with no easy answers;
       through failing where we hoped to succeed and making an
       impact when we felt useless;
       through the patience and the dreams and the love of others;
and through Jesus Christ and his Spirit, you keep us.

Allegiances
Jeff Dols

I pledge allegiance to the Cross
of Jesus of Nazareth, the Christ,
and to the Kingdom for which it stands,
one Creation under God, indivisible,
with Unconditional Love and Justice for all.

Loving Jesus,
You became one of us to reveal to us the heart of God
and to call us to be the Body of Christ in our world.
You saved the world by showing us the meaning of mercy,
forgiveness, and unconditional love,
and then sacrificing your life to show us the way to transformation.

Help us to be mindful when we pledge allegiance to God and country
that we keep them in the right order.
And help to remove our blindness,
when we fail to see the times when allegiance to the other
is in direct conflict with allegiance to the One.

The Idol of Self
Archbishop Oscar Romero

We must overturn so many idols,
the idol of self first of all,
so that we can be humble,
and only from our humility
can learn to be redeemers,
can learn to work together
in the way the world really needs.
Liberation that raises a cry against others
is no true liberation.
Liberation that means revolutions of hate and violence
and takes the lives of others
or abases the dignity of others
cannot be true liberty.
True liberty does violence to self
and, like Christ,
who disregarded that he was sovereign,
becomes a slave to serve others.

Justice and Charity: A Parable
Ronald Rolheiser

There is a story told, now quite famous within social justice circles:

Once upon a time there was a town that was built just beyond the bend of large river. One day some of the children from the town were playing beside the river when they noticed three bodies floating in the water. They ran for help and the townsfolk quickly pulled the bodies out of the river.

One body was dead so they buried it. One was alive, but quite ill, so they put that person into the hospital. The third turned out to be a healthy child, who they then placed with a family who cared for it and who took it to school.

From that day on, every day a number of bodies came floating down the river and, every day, the good people of the town would pull them out and tend to them—taking the sick to hospitals, placing the children with families, and burying those who were dead.

This went on for years; each day brought its quota of bodies, and the townsfolk not only came to expect a number of bodies each day but also worked at developing more elaborate systems for picking them out of the river and tending to them. Some of the townsfolk became quite generous in tending to these bodies and a few extraordinary ones even gave up their jobs so that they could tend to this concern full-time. And the town itself felt a certain healthy pride in its generosity.

However, during all these years and despite all that generosity and effort, nobody thought to go up the river, beyond the bend that hid from their sight what was above them, and find out why, daily, those bodies came floating down the river.

Morning Prayer
Macrina Wiederkehr, O.S.B.

O Radiant Dawn,
O Loving God,
as the day begins to tell of your glory
etch into our hearts a bit of heaven
that we may take your shining light
wherever we go.

Shine on us, in us,
and through us
just as your sun shines in the sky.

Give us enough of your light
that we may see the new
greening power
within us.

Give us
enough lightning and storms
to shake up our soil,
enough wind to keep us spirited,
enough death to bring us life,
and enough goodness
to help us remember who we are.

With trust,
we expect this prayer
to come true in our lives
for it is in the name of Jesus
that we pray. Amen.

Believe

Joan Metzner, M.M.

Believe in your questions,
        no matter how trifling.
They are the gateway to knowledge,
        wisdom and enlightenment.

Believe in your gifts,
        no matter how small.
They are God's providence
        to your world,
            to enrich it, to ennoble it,
            to bring it love.

Believe in your past,
        no matter how painful.
It is a unique book of history:
        Gospel Revelation of God's
        mercy and faithfulness.

Believe in your yearnings,
        no matter how subtle.
They are energy, urging you
        forward
            in your quest for God.

Believe in your goodness,
        no matter pointed fingers.
They are only passing vestiges
        of fear
            reminding you to forgive,
            to remain rooted in Love's
            Reality.

Believe in your vision,
        no matter the climb.
It is a mountainpeak,
            calling you to
            experience God.

Believe in your decisions,
            no matter the mistakes.
They are your "Yes" to life,
                your assent to the Field,
                where God is to be found.

Believe in your ideas,
            no matter the doubts.
They are seeds, seeking nourishment,
                sunshine, live-giving water.

Believe in your neighbors,
            no matter the risk.
They are sent from God
            to walk with you.

Believe in your God,
            no matter the mist.
God is strong and trustworthy
            and God cares for you.

Prayer for Results
Saint Thomas More

Lord, give me the grace to bring about the things that I pray for.

Social Action
Rabbi Jack Riemer

We cannot merely pray to You, O God, to end war:
For we know You made the world in a way
That we must find our own path of peace
Within ourselves and with our neighbor.

We cannot merely pray to You, O God, to root out prejudice:
For You have already given us eyes
With which to see the good in all people
If we would only use them rightly.

We cannot merely pray to You, O God, to end starvation:
For You have already given us the resources
With which to feed the entire world
If we would only use them wisely.

We cannot merely pray to You, O God, to end despair:
For You have already given us the power
To clear away slums and to give hope
If we would only use our power justly.

We cannot merely pray to You, O God, to end disease:
For You have already given us great minds
With which to search out cures and healing
If we would only use them constructively.

Therefore we pray to You, instead O God,
For strength, determination, and will power,
To *do* instead of just to pray
To *become* instead of merely to wish.

CHAPTER EIGHT

"Call the Sabbath a Delight and the Holy Day of the LORD Honorable"
(Isaiah 58:13)

Holy Days, Holidays and Feast Days

The Work of Christmas
Howard Thurman

When the song of the angel is stilled,
When the star in the sky is gone,
When the kings and princes are home,
When the shepherds are back with their flock,
The work of Christmas begins:
To find the lost,
To heal the broken,
To feed the hungry,
To release the prisoner,
To rebuild the nations,
To bring peace among others
To make music in the heart.

Prayer for Peace to Mary, the Light of Hope
Pope John Paul II

Immaculate Heart of Mary,
help us to conquer the menace of evil,
which so easily takes root in the hearts of the people of today,
and whose immeasurable effects
already weigh down upon our modern world
and seem to block the paths toward the future.
From famine and war, deliver us. From nuclear war, from
    incalculable self destruction, from every kind of war, deliver us.
From sins against human life from its very beginning, deliver us.
From hatred and from the demeaning of the dignity of the children
    of God, deliver us.
From every kind of injustice in the life of society, both national and
    international, deliver us.
From readiness to trample on the commandments of God, deliver us.
From attempts to stifle in human hearts the very truth of God,
    deliver us.
From the loss of awareness of good and evil, deliver us.
From sins against the Holy Spirit, deliver us.
Accept, O Mother of Christ,
this cry laden with the sufferings of all individual human beings,
laden with the sufferings of whole societies.
Help us with the power of the Holy Spirit conquer all sin:
individual sin and the "sin of the world,"
sin in all its manifestations.
Let there be revealed once more in the history of the world
the infinite saving power of the redemption:
the power of the merciful love.
May it put a stop to evil.
May it transform consciences.
May your Immaculate Heart reveal for all the light of hope. Amen.

Prayer at Election Time
Sisters of Mercy

Loving and gracious God, we remember that your plan for us is fullness of life lived with love, justice and mercy.

Be with us and our whole nation this year as we work together in selecting political leaders at all levels of our society. Help us keep the common good before us.

Strengthen our gifts of wisdom, courage and respect for the views of others.

Deepen in us the willingness to act in solidarity with people who are economically poor and with women seeking fullness of life in society.

Help us be persistent in testing political remedies against what they will do for people, to people, with people, and what they will mean for the health of our earth home.

Help us to support one another in exercising our precious responsibilities as citizens in a representative democracy.

After the elections, strengthen us to continue to work with our leaders, seeking an ever more just society that acts in harmony and interdependence with all creation.

We ask this in the name of Jesus in union with Your Spirit. Amen.

To Those Who Are Hungry
Catholic Relief Services

God our Creator,
to those who are hungry and thirsty,
give food and drink.

To those who are not hungry and thirsty,
give a hunger and a thirst for justice.

Help us to share in the creation of a more just and peaceful world.

Bless the Lenten alms we set aside in our household
for the good of any sister or brother in need.

We pray through Christ the Lord.

Amen.

Prayer for Martin Luther King's Birthday
Attributed to J-Glenn Murray, S.J.

O Guardian of Israel,
Our shelter and shade,
Stir up in us that flame of justice
That Jesus incited on this earth,
That rages in our hearts by the Holy Spirit.
O arouse in us
That very flame of righteousness
That enticed Martin
To be a living sacrifice of praise,
To seek freedom for all God's children.
O to you, God ever faithful and true,
Be glory for ever and ever.
Amen.

A Prayer for the Beginning of Easter
Jan L. Richardson

God of community,
who calls us to be in relationship
with one another
and who has promised to dwell
wherever two or three are gathered,
hear this prayer:

By your Spirit you have graced each of us
with differing gifts.
To one you have given the speaking of wisdom,
to another, the utterance of knowledge,
to another, faith,
to another, gifts of healing,
to another, the working of miracles,
to another, prophesy,
to another, discernment of spirits,
to another, various kinds of tongues,
and to another, the interpretation of tongues.
(1 Corinthians 12:7–11)

For these and all gifts
by which you bless our communities,
I give you thanks.

And for any way in which I have shared
in deepening the wounds of the body of Christ
I seek your love-filled forgiveness.

Open my eyes, O God, to perceive the gifts
you have placed within me
and to honor the differing gifts
which my sisters and brothers offer.
Bless our hands, our hearts, our vision
to work together for the bringing of your kindom,
that in our differences, we may find grace;
in our laboring, we may find justice;
in our suffering, hope;
in our embracing, love;
and in our risking, transformation.

By these acts may we bring healing
to the tender, wounded, and strong
body of Christ,
rising in our midst.

Note: "Kindom" denotes a world in which we recognize that we are related, that we are "kin" in God, and work to build relationships of love, peace and justice with all of creation.

On This Memorial Day

Jane Deren

On this Memorial Day
Grant peace to the souls
of all those soldiers who died in war.
We remember the tears and grief of their families,
The pain of mothers, wives, husbands and children
Who lost precious loved ones.

To build a meaningful memorial to them,
We ask God to give us all the will
To work for peace around the world
So no more sons, daughters, husbands, wives, fathers, nor mothers
Are slaughtered by the guns and bombs of war.

We ask Mary, who held the lifeless body of her son
And was pierced by the sorrow of his suffering and death,
To grant us the compassion and wisdom to affirm life
And honor the dead through forgiveness and peace making.

May God have mercy on the souls of the departed.
Grant them peace, O Lord.

May we have mercy on the living.
Grant us peace, O Lord.
In Your name we pray.
Amen.

CHAPTER NINE

"Call to Me and I Will Answer You" (Jeremiah 33:3)

Prayer Services

Dorothy Day, Servant of God
A Catholic Worker for Justice and Peace

—*Dr. Edward Francis Gabriele*

Dorothy Day (1897–1980) confronted the consciences of Americans, especially Catholics, to see the radical implications of a Gospel commitment to justice and peace. After embracing Catholicism, Day founded the Catholic Worker Movement with Peter Maurin, and she started *The Catholic Worker* newspaper, which was intended to comfort the afflicted and afflict the comfortable. She started the first House of Hospitality to offer food, clothing, and shelter to poor people. Day steadfastly opposed war through her nonviolent protests. Dorothy Day indeed gave new meaning to what it means to be holy: combining unity with the poor and service to them, struggling for justice, offering compassionate hospitality, integrating ministry and prayer. Her life is a living parable of active love and faith in Christ Jesus.

Morning
Call to Prayer
As daylight breaks, the truth of the Gospel again dispels the darkness of night. Each day God calls us to a deeper faith in Christ Jesus. Each day God asks that we give flesh again to the Word who is our life. This day we remember the life and work of Dorothy Day. We are moved by her prophetic sacrifices for the poor and the oppressed. With her we pray for the increased commitment to building God's Reign in our midst by our renewed deeds of justice and peace for those who have no advocates.

Praise
All honor and praise be yours,
almighty and ever living God.

Each day your Spirit rouses us from sleep
to put on the armor of light
and go forth to proclaim the truth of the Gospel
in deeds of mercy, justice, and peace.
As daylight breaks, you bid us give flesh
to the Word, who is our life and freedom.
With saints and ancients of every time and place,
you bid us preach the Gospel by our deeds of justice
and thereby be your instruments of peace
until the last darkness of human oppression has been dispelled.

Reading (from Dorothy Day)
An understanding of the dogma of the Mystical Body is perhaps the
greatest need of the present time. It is a further explanation of the
Incarnation....
Christ is the head and we are the members. And the illnesses of
injustice, hate, disunion, race hatred, prejudice, class war,
selfishness, greed, nationalism, and war weaken this Mystical Body,
just as prayer and sacrifices of countless of the faithful strengthen it....
All men are our neighbors and Christ told us we should love our
neighbors, whether they be friend or enemy.

Acclamations
In celebration we call to mind the life and witness of Dorothy Day
who called the church of Christ to a new dawning of peace and
justice as the hallmark of a Gospel life. With her and all the saints,
we celebrate the price of the Gospel in our life. In joy we pray:
Honor, love, and praise be yours!
- We worship you, God, who created us for freedom and for
  loving, as we pray...
- We honor you, God, who opens our eyes to the needs of the
  poor and the oppressed, as we pray...

- We bless the presence of the Merciful One, who strengthens and empowers our hands for works of peace, as we pray...
- We are grateful for the presence of the Spirit, who enlivens us in hope until that day when the fullness of peace shall dawn, as we pray...

Closing

Gracious and merciful God, you do not wish your beloved children to wander in loneliness and pain. As Jesus did, you call us always to minister to those whose hunger and thirst for justice and peace are insatiable. With Dorothy Day and all the saints, strengthen our heart and hands for the service of the poor, until that day when the fullness of your justice and peace will flower. We ask this as all things through Jesus our Messiah forever and ever. Amen.

Evening

Call to Prayer

With the coming of the night, we open our self to the light of Christ heard in the cries of the poor. Millions wander in hopeless poverty and are tempted to despair. For them Christ kindles a lamp in our midst to light our way to love tenderly, act justly, and walk humbly. This night we pray for and with Dorothy Day and all those who work for justice and peace. With them we are joined forever in the challenge of the Gospel to preach a year of jubilee by liberating every prisoner of poverty and fear.

Thanksgiving

O God who moves with brilliant love
in the shades of the evening,
from the simple elegance of earth
you fashioned our heart for love and dignity.
From long ago you taught us
that you are most manifest

in the lives of the poor and those who need our love.
This night and forever,
with Dorothy Day and all people of justice,
you bid us go forth into the night
and search out those whose lives are seared
by the angry wounds of poverty and despair.
For them you ask us to light the lamp of justice
by feeding their needs and tending their wounds.
You are the strength that makes bold our hands
for the works of loving justice.
You are the comfort that tends our fears.
You are the brilliance that leads us on in hope
until the final coming of Christ's justice and peace.

Reading (from Dorothy Day)
It is no use saying that we are born two thousand years too late to give room to Christ.... Christ is always with us, always asking for room in our hearts.
But now it is with the voice of our contemporaries that He speaks, with the eyes of store clerks, factory workers, and children that he gazes; with the hands of office workers, slum dwellers, and suburban housewives that He gives.... And giving shelter or food to anyone who asks for it, or needs it, is giving to Christ.

Intercessions
We are grateful for the witness of heroic Christians who remind us that a commitment to the Gospel of Christ is a commitment to justice and peace. With Dorothy Day and all who minister to the poor, we offer our needs to God as we pray: *Keep us mindful of your love.*

- For all Christians, that the spirit of God may make us ever mindful of our call to serve the needs of all God's people, let us pray...

- For all those who have embraced a life of voluntary poverty so as to serve the needs of the poor and lowly, let us pray...
- For all those whose lives prophetically challenge the spirit of complacency and selfishness in society, let us pray...
- For the poor and the dispossessed, for the fearful and the suffering, that our deeds of mercy may be their comfort, let us pray...

Closing Prayer
Gracious and merciful God, you do not wish your beloved children to wander in loneliness and pain. As Jesus did, you call us always to minister to those whose hunger and thirst for justice and peace are insatiable. With Dorothy Day and all the saints, strengthen our heart and hands for the service of the poor, until that day when the fullness of your justice and peace will flower. We ask this as all things through Jesus our Messiah forever and ever. Amen.

Farmer's Prayer Service

Leader: May the Lord grant us an open spirit, and an open heart to hear and to share and to be granted a hope-filled spirit.

All: Hear us, O Lord.

Reader: Isaiah 53:1–7

Silence

Reader: 1 Peter 2:21–24

Silence

Reader: Psalm 25:1–11

Litany
Divine Shepherd, bring your scattered sheep home.
Divine Mender, call our sins never to mind.
Divine Surgeon, reset our broken heart in love.
Divine Counselor, share your tender feelings of compassion.
Divine Father, tell us again the story of your son.
Divine Mediator, arbitrate our hatred and our wars.
Divine King, govern our complex impulses and motives.
Divine Prophet, proclaim your justice to all the nations.
Divine Savior, heal our fragile, weary world.
Divine Spirit, grant us trust and joy.

Leader: Let us pray. Lord, you have planted your love in the smallest of all packages. May we be fertile soil so that our human experiences may bear fruit to nourish the hungry, comfort the oppressed, bring home the alienated. May your kingdom come. May your truth, justice, love and peace reign. Amen.

A Litany for World Peace

Leader: Remember, O Lord, the peoples of the world divided into many nations and tongues; deliver us from every evil which obstructs thy saving purpose, and fulfill thy promises of old to establish thy kingdom of peace.

From the curse of war and all that begets it,
Response: *O Lord, deliver us.*

From believing and speaking lies against other nations,
O Lord, deliver us.

From narrow loyalties and selfish isolation,
O Lord, deliver us.

From fear and distrust of other nations, from all false pride, vainglory, and self-conceit,
O Lord, deliver us.

From the lust of the mighty for riches, that drives peaceful peoples to slaughter,
O Lord, deliver us.

From putting our trust in the weapons of war, and from want of faith in the power of justice and goodwill,
O Lord, deliver us.

From every thought, word, and deed which divides the human family and separates us from the perfect realization of thy love,
O Lord, deliver us.

Leader: Eternal God, who showest thy people the way in which they should go, turn our feet from the city of destruction toward the city of God, and redirect our desires and labors in accordance with thy will; that we may achieve the new world for which thy Son was content to die, even Jesus Christ our Lord.

That nations may vie with each other in the service of all and not in seeking dominion,
Response: *O God, we pray thee.*

That science may be the constant handmaid of life and never the henchman of death,
O God, we pray thee.

That the treasure now spent on the engines of war may be used for the arts of peace,
O God, we pray thee.

That the people may rejoice to endure labor and want and death to win, not a war, but thy kingdom,
O God, we pray thee.

That we may love not only our country but also the whole family of nations,
O God, we pray thee.

That ancient enmities may pass away and that thou wilt make all things new,
O God, we pray thee.

Leader: O Christ, at whose word the wind and waves were still, rebuke, we pray thee, our violence and usher in the day of genuine peace; that we may truly serve thee, who with the creator God and the Holy Spirit liveth and worketh for us unceasingly, now and forever.

Lord of life, master of all, pattern of gentleness,
Hear us, Lord Jesus.

By the prophets' dream of old,
Grant us victory over war.

By the angels' song of peace,
Raise up leaders of goodwill.

By thy gospel's words of love,
Help us to love our enemies.

By thy sacrificial death,
Teach the nations self-denial.

By the kingdom thou has promised,
Make the nations one.

Leader: God of the future years, we pray for all thy family upon the earth and for every agency of world cooperation that it may grow in usefulness and power:

For thy universal Church,
Response: *We beseech thee.*

For the world organization of nations,
We beseech thee.

For international federations of labor, industry, and commerce,
We beseech thee.

For the departments of state, for all ambassadors, ministers, and diplomats,
We beseech thee.

For the prophets and pioneers who have seen the promised land afar off and dedicated their lives to its service,
We beseech thee.

For the common folk in every land who live in peace and quietness,
We beseech thee.

Eternal God, unto thee we commit ourselves; use even us with our ignorance and frailty to accomplish thy holy will; and hasten the day when all shall dwell together in mutual helpfulness and love; for thine is the kingdom, the power, and the glory, forever. Amen.

Isaiah Prayer Service
Isaiah 58:6–11

Call to Worship

Leader: Let us recall that God is our light and our hope, our refuge and our strength. Let us be attentive to God's presence with us. May we listen with open minds and hearts to the words of God.

Responsive Reading

Leader: Is this not the fast that I choose:

People: To loose the bonds of injustice, to undo the thongs of the yoke, to let the oppressed go free, and to break every yoke?

Leader: Is it not to share your bread with the hungry, and to bring the homeless poor into your house; When you see the naked, to cover them, and not to hide yourself from your own kin?

People: Then your light shall break forth like the dawn, and your healing shall spring up quickly. Your vindication shall go before you, the glory of the Lord shall be your rear guard.

Leader: Then shall you call, and the Lord will answer; you shall cry for help and he will answer: Here I am!

People: If you remove the yoke from among you, the pointing of the finger, the speaking of evil,

Leader: If you offer your food to the hungry and satisfy the needs of the afflicted,

People: Then your light shall rise in the darkness and your gloom be like the noonday.

Leader: The Lord will guide you continually, and satisfy your needs in parched places, and make your bones strong; and you shall be like a watered garden, like a spring of water, whose waters never fail.

Prayer Service Based on the Seven Themes of Catholic Social Teaching
Catholic Diocese of Richmond

Our Call, Our Tradition
Leader: Let us place ourselves in the presence of the God who calls us to be salt and light.

Reader: Matthew 5:14–16

All: The Church's social teaching is a rich treasure of wisdom about building a just society and living lives of holiness amidst the challenges of modern society.

Life and Dignity of the Human Person
Reader: Genesis 1:27

All: The Catholic Church proclaims that human life is sacred and that the dignity of the human person is the foundation of a moral vision for society.... We believe that...the measure of every institution is whether it threatens or enhances the life and dignity of the human person.

Call to Family, Community and Participation
Reader: Exodus 6:7

All: The person is not only sacred but also social. How we organize our society in economics and politics, in law and policy directly affects human dignity and the capacity of individuals to grow in community.

Human Rights and Responsibilities
Reader: Isaiah 10:1–2

All: The Catholic tradition teaches that human dignity can be protected and a healthy community can be achieved only if human rights are protected and responsibilities are met. Therefore, every person has a fundamental right to life and a right to those things required for human decency.

Option for the Poor and Vulnerable
Reader: Acts 2:44–45

All: A basic moral test is how our most vulnerable members are faring. In a society marred by deepening divisions between rich and poor, our tradition…instructs us to put the needs of the poor and vulnerable first.

The Dignity of Work and the Rights of Workers
Reader: Sirach 34:22

All: The economy must serve people…. Work is more than a way to make a living; it is a form of continuing participation in God's creation. If the dignity of work is to be protected, then the basic rights of workers must be respected.

Global Solidarity
Reader: Micah 4:3

All: We are our brothers' and sisters' keepers…. We are one human family, whatever our national, racial, ethnic, economic, and ideological differences. Learning to practice the virtue of solidarity means learning that "loving our neighbor" has global dimensions in an interdependent world.

Care for God's Creation
Reader: Genesis 1:31

All: We show our respect for the Creator by our stewardship of creation…. We are called to protect people and the planet, living our faith in relationship with all God's creation. This environmental challenge has fundamental moral and ethical dimensions that cannot be ignored.

Seeing as God Sees

Reader: John 9:39–41

Leader: Our tradition calls us to see the world in new ways—to reject the blindness of our age. And so we pray. We are called to see with the eyes of the poor in a world blinded by riches and power.

All: Cure our blindness, O God.

Leader: We are called to see with the eyes of the outcast, the leper, the person with AIDS in a world blinded by fear.

All: Cure our blindness, O God.

Leader: We are called to see with the eyes of all God's creatures in a world blind to the beauty of God's creation.

All: Cure our blindness, O God.

Leader: Jesus has opened our eyes to the needs of God's world.

All: We are ready to open our hands to God's work.

Leader: Jesus has opened our minds to the injustice of the world.

All: We are ready to open our mouths to proclaim God's justice.

The Great Prayer of the Church
From the Liturgy of Saint John Chrysostom

Leader: In peace let us pray to the Lord.
All: *Lord have mercy.*

For the peace from above, and for our salvation, let us pray
to the Lord.
Lord have mercy.

For the peace of the whole world; for the welfare of the holy
churches of God, and for the unity of all people, let us pray
to the Lord.
Lord have mercy.

For this holy community of faith, and for those who with faith,
reverence and love of God enter herein, let us pray to the Lord.
Lord have mercy.

For our pastors, for all clergy, for all who bear office in the church,
for all of the people of God in all times and places, let us pray
to the Lord.
Lord have mercy.

For the President of the United States of America and for all civil
authorities, for the leaders of all nations and for those who serve in
the United Nations, let us pray to the Lord.
Lord have mercy.

That God will aid them and grant them wisdom and strength to
struggle for justice and peace.
Lord have mercy.

For this community, and for every city and land, and for the faithful
who dwell in them, let us pray to the Lord.
Lord have mercy.

For healthful seasons, for abundance of the fruits of the earth and for peaceful times, let us pray to the Lord.
Lord have mercy.

For travelers by sea, by land and by air; for the sick and the suffering; for refugees and the homeless; for prisoners and their salvation; for the poor and the needy, let us pray to the Lord.
Lord have mercy.

For our deliverance from all tribulation, wrath, danger and necessity, let us pray to the Lord.
Lord have mercy.

Help us; save us; have mercy upon us and keep us, O God, by your grace.
Lord have mercy.

Calling to remembrance our mothers and fathers in the faith, with all of God's saints let us commend ourselves and each other, and all our lives unto Christ our God.
To you, O Lord.

O Lord our God, whose power is beyond anything that we can imagine, whose glory is greater than our ability to know, whose mercy knows no limits and whose love toward humankind is deeper than our capacity to understand: Do, O Master, in your tender compassion look upon us and upon this holy community of faith and grant us and those who pray with us your rich blessings and benefits. For unto you are due all glory, honor and worship: to the Father, and to the Son, and to the Holy Spirit: now and ever and unto ages of ages. Amen.

A Lord's Prayer for Justice
Ronald Rolheiser

Our Father... Who always stands with the weak, the powerless, the poor, the abandoned, the sick, the aged, the very young, the unborn, and those who, by victim of circumstance, beat the heat of the day.

Who art in heaven... where everything will be reversed, where the first will be last and the last will be first, but where all will be well and every manner of being will be well.

Hallowed be thy name... may we always acknowledge your holiness, respecting that your ways are not our ways, your standards are not our standards. May the reverence we give your name pull us out of the selfishness that prevents us from seeing the pain of our neighbor.

Your Kingdom come... help us to create a world where, beyond our own needs and hurts, we will do justice, love tenderly and walk humbly with you and each other.

Your will be done... open our freedom to let you in so that the complete mutuality that characterizes your life might flow through our veins and thus the life that we help generate may radiate your equal love for all and your special love for the poor.

On earth as in heaven... may the work of our hands, the temples and structures we build in this world, reflect the temple and the structure of your glory so that the joy, graciousness, tenderness, and justice of heaven will show forth within all of our structures on earth.

Give... life and love to us and help us to see always everything as a gift. Help us to know that nothing comes to us by right and that we must give because we have been given to. Help us realize that we must give to the poor, not because they need it, but because our own health depends upon our giving to them.

*Us...*the truly plural us. Give not just to our own but to everyone, including those who are very different than the narrow us. Give your gifts to all of us equally.

*This day...*not tomorrow. Do not let us push things off into some indefinite future so that we can continue to live justified lives in the face of injustice because we can make good excuses for our inactivity.

*Our daily bread...*so that each person in the world may have enough food, enough clean water, enough clean air, adequate health care, and sufficient access to education so as to have the sustenance for a healthy life. Teach us to give from our sustenance and not just from our surplus.

*And forgive us our trespasses...*forgive us our blindness toward our neighbor, our self-preoccupation, our racism, our sexism, and our incurable propensity to worry only about ourselves and our own. Forgive us our capacity to watch the evening news and do nothing about it.

*As we forgive those who trespass against us...*help us to forgive those who victimize us. Help us to mellow out in spirit, to not grow bitter with age, to forgive the imperfect parents and systems that wounded, cursed and ignored us.

*And do not put us to the test...*do not judge us only by whether we have fed the hungry, given clothing to the naked, visited the sick, or tried to mend the systems that victimized the poor. Spare us this test for none of us can stand before your gospel scrutiny. Give us, instead, more days to mend our ways, our selfishness, and our systems.

*But deliver us from evil...*that is, from the blindness that lets us continue to participate in anonymous systems within which we need not see who gets less as we get more.

Amen.

The Lord's Prayer: An Adaptation
Jane Deren

Leader: Our God who is in heaven
and in all of us here on earth;
the hungry, the oppressed, the excluded. Holy is your name.

All: *May your reign come.*

May your reign come and your will be done;
in our choice to struggle with the complexities of this world
and to confront greed and the desire for power in ourselves,
in our nation and in the global community.

May your reign come.

Give us this day our daily bread;
bread that we are called to share,
bread that you have given us abundantly
and that we must distribute fairly, ensuring security for all.

May your reign come.

Forgive us our trespasses;
times we have turned away from the struggles
of other people and countries,
times we have thought only of our own security.

May your reign come.

Lead us not into temptation;
the temptation to close our minds, ears, and eyes
to the unfair global systems that create
larger and larger gaps between the rich and the poor;
the temptation to think it is too difficult
to bring about more just alternatives.

May your reign come.

Deliver us from evil;
the evil of a world where violence happens in your name,
where wealth for a few is more important
than economic rights for all,
where gates and barriers between people
are so hard to bring down.

May your reign come.

May your reign come, for yours is the kingdom,
the power and the glory forever and ever. Amen.

Justice Stations of the Cross
John Bucki, S.J.

1. Jesus is condemned to death.
Jesus is trapped by the same system that brings us the death penalty, the harshness of life in prison, political prisoners, torture, white collar crime, racial profiling, the criminalization of the poor, and all of the inequities of our world's criminal justice systems.

2. Jesus is made to carry his cross.
Jesus carries his burden as do all those who work the land, labor for low wages, struggle to find work, care for their children and family, worry over their debts, strive for their children, attend poor schools, are abused by their bosses, or in any way struggle to make it in this world.

3. Jesus falls the first time.
The burden that crushes Jesus can be compared to the burdens of today—the burden of debt that crushes the poor economies of the world, the unequal distribution of resources which stifles development for many people and nations.

4. Jesus meets his mother.
Jesus looks on his mother with love and sees all the pain and possibility of relationship, deep family love and fidelity, abuse and violence, mutual loving care, separation and divorce, loneliness and community.

5. Simon helps Jesus carry his cross.
Jesus' story becomes Simon's story as well. Globalization can be both a burden and a relief, a freedom and a limit. Jesus and Simon are both victims and helpers. Good and evil play out as their lives are connected.

6. Jesus falls the second time.
The burden that crushes Jesus is unfair, as are the economic and political inequalities of our day—wages, resources, schools, rights, power, savings, taxes. Our systems are often unfair.

7. Veronica wipes the face of Jesus.
This "small" act of charity is a most wonderful action of great compassion. It seems to be all that Veronica can do at the moment, yet the injustice remains. She cannot stop the suffering of Jesus. The compassion of Veronica calls out for social change, for an end to injustice, for a new way of living together.

8. Jesus comforts the women of Jerusalem.
Women bear the burdens of the world in a special way. They disproportionately struggle under the injustices of our systems. The experience of women throughout the ages calls us to end the injustices. It calls us to a new heaven and a new earth, to a new way of being sisters and brothers.

9. Jesus falls the third time.
The burden that crushes Jesus is like the burden of materialism. Every time the world worships things before people, power before justice, and consumption before the spirit, we lose what it means to be human and alive.

10. Jesus is stripped of his garments.
This radical loss of everything continues to be felt in the lives of all the poor—those without enough food, clothing, shelter, education, respect, dignity, human rights and community.

11. Jesus is nailed to the cross.
Jesus is a person of active nonviolence, yet here he comes to know violence against his person—the same violence that is seen in our wars and preparation for war, in the violence on our streets and in

our homes, in our weapons of mass destruction, in ethnic cleansing, in genocide, in all these countless examples of violence.

12. Jesus dies on the cross.
Power and control are dominant values in our world, yet Jesus loses all of these things that the world considers important. But at the same time, in Jesus nailed to a cross, we see a person of great freedom and compassionate love and a special awesome power—the power of the suffering God crying out for justice.

13. Jesus is taken down from the cross.
Jesus is radically stripped of everything. He is a human person whose rights and dignity have been taken away. In Jesus, we see all the women and men of our world who still seek their basic human rights—the right to food, water, clothing, shelter, education, political freedom, development, justice, etc.

14. Jesus is placed in the tomb.
Jesus is carefully placed into the earth, an earth that is the divine creation, a planet that we so often abuse as we waste resources, as we seek profit before all else, as we consume without awareness, and as we disrespect the awesome beauty that is God's gift.

The Way of the Cross of a Migrant

1. Jesus is condemned to death.
Reader 1: Jesus, you are sentenced unjustly by your enemies. I know what you must feel. Many of us have been condemned to a slow death, because of thinking and because of taking our inspiration from the Bible and its message. Our children are already condemned to death because they carry on their backs part of the external debt, condemned to die because of the deterioration of health services, condemned to die illiterate because education is becoming the privilege of the few.
Reader 2: Jesus is unjustly condemned.
All: Help us, who have been unjustly condemned.

2. Jesus carries his cross.
Reader 1: Jesus, you accepted the cross for us. I also have many crosses, seven crosses of responsibility, to be exact, seven children to raise without a father, without a husband, and without any help. Seven children suffering from malnutrition. Thanks be to God, I have obtained, if only for three months, a job as a domestic, which will allow me to survive and keep them alive.
Reader 2: Jesus, we need your help to be able to go on.
All: Give us the faith to not come disheartened.

3. Jesus falls the first time.
Reader 1: Jesus falls under the weight of the cross. Help us not to fall under the weight of our crosses of each day: poverty, discouragement, ups and downs, a lack of hope. We the migrants go from one side to the other in this country and, because many times we have fallen, we are not welcome.
Reader 2: Lord, you fell under the weight of the cross.
All: Help us not to be bitter.

4. Jesus meets his mother.
Reader 1: The eyes of Jesus and those of his mother meet. I
remember the last time I saw my family. I also remember the
hopeful aspect of those of us who went out in search of a better
future. I knew the way would be long and uncertain.
Reader 2: Mother, patron of those tempted by despair,
All: Help us to find in your face the comfort Jesus found there.

5. Simon, the Cyrene, helps Jesus carry the cross.
Reader 1: They say that Simon was converted after helping Jesus
with the cross. Jesus, please convert me while I carry my crosses
with yours. Let us not fall in our search and lead us to conversion,
following the example of so many others who do not grow weak in
the struggle.
Reader 2: Jesus, helped by Simon,
All: Teach us to carry our cross with dignity.

6. Veronica wipes the face of Jesus.
Reader 1: Veronica sees your bleeding face. She wipes it with her
new handkerchief. So the impression of your face remains on the
handkerchief, but even more, your suffering is imprinted on her
heart. I remember the suffering face of so many migrants that I meet
in the city.
Reader 2: Lord Jesus, who suffered so much injustice,
All: Impregnate our hearts and our lives with your love and your
strength.

7. Jesus falls the second time.
Reader 1: Jesus, the weight of the cross is too much and you fall
again. My cross is very heavy, also, Lord. It is so hard. People call me
"vagrant" and "lazy" as if I were a criminal. I want to return to my
town, but I cannot, because the situation there has become even
worse.
Reader 2: Jesus who got up the second time,

All: Don't let them marginalize me because of my condition as a migrant.

8. Jesus speaks to the women of Jerusalem.

Reader 1: Jesus, you are suffering, but even so you speak to the women of Jerusalem who weep and who know your pain. You comfort them. Jesus, we need you, still today, to speak to these women who suffer, to these women who weep to see their children eating so little or working in the streets under inhuman conditions. We need you to speak to the women who have to sell their bodies in order to survive or who are exploited at their work.

Reader 2: Jesus, you who comforted the women of Jerusalem,

All: Comfort today also those who weep.

9. Jesus falls the third time.

Reader 1: Jesus, your cross is so heavy, like mine, but you inspire me to continue on. My cross becomes so heavy when they tell me, "There is no work here. Return to your town, to your country, because here you are a nuisance." And I can't do anything in the face of this.

Reader 2: Lord, forgive them.

All: Because they know not what they do.

10. Jesus is stripped of his garments.

Reader 1: Jesus, you lost the very last of your possessions. They have taken everything from me, also: the land that I worked, the trust in the organization that worked for my rights, the possibility of having access to health and education services.

Reader 2: Jesus, stay with me and help us not to fall into the pit of despair.

All: Help those of us who have nothing except our faith.

11. Jesus is nailed to the cross.

Reader 1: Jesus, it is so cruel and unjust, what they did to you. Now they nail us, the migrants, to the cross of poverty, of marginalization, of ignorance and of the scarce opportunities for work. I have so many questions to ask: Why so many loans of millions of dollars? Why spend so much money on arms and armies? Why do only some have access to health, education and work?

Reader 2: Jesus, you were the first to combat despair.

All: Help us not to despair.

12. Jesus dies on the cross.

Reader 1: Jesus, on your cross you united the divine with the human. You died accused of inciting the people, of being political, of being revolutionary. If you began a revolution, it was a revolution of love. Don't allow us to die, hating.

Reader 2: Jesus, you gave your life for us, but not in vain.

All: May the life of so many migrant brothers and sisters not be in vain.

13. Jesus is taken down from the cross.

Reader 1: Your mutilated body is taken down from the cross and placed in the arms of your mother. Jesus, I know what a mutilated body is. I have held in my arms the body of a friend who was assaulted and killed when we tried to come to the United States. What can we do? We have to have faith that death is not in vain and believe in the resurrection.

Reader 2: Jesus, mutilated by soldiers,

All: Teach us to forgive those in this society who mutilate our hope, our dreams and our bodies.

14. Jesus is buried in the tomb.

Reader 1: Those whom you loved so much buried you. They can return your body to the earth, but they cannot destroy your spirit. You will rise. You give us the hope that we also will be raised from the dead.

Reader 2: Jesus, who died and rose from the dead,

All: Help us to have faith in your death and resurrection.

15. Resurrection.

Reader 1: They killed the body but they cannot kill the spirit. Jesus, you said, "I am the resurrection and the life." Help us to have the strength to continue our journey, to fight against despair, to be freed from oppression and from sin.

Reader 2: We adore you, O Christ, and we bless you.

All: Because by your holy cross you have redeemed the world.

The Way of the Cross With Oscar Romero

1. Jesus is condemned to death.

Luke 23:1–2, 5–6

This is a God who renounces his condition as God, coming down
from the happiness of heaven to become a man, a man who doesn't
go around mentioning his prerogative as God—"any man," says the
Bible today. "Any man" who is tied to the authority of his time and
carried to the courts. When Saint Paul says "any man," it occurs to
me to think of those people whom we are already accustomed to
seeing in our newspapers: the handcuffed peasant, the tortured
peasant, the laborer whose rights aren't recognized. This is the "any
man" that Christ wanted to become. (March 19, 1978)

2. Jesus takes the cross upon his shoulders.

John 19:16–17

We feel in the Christ of Holy Week, with the cross upon his
shoulders, that this is the people who are also carrying their cross.
We feel the people crucified in this Christ with the open arms
crucified, but it is from this Christ that a people crucified and
humiliated will encounter their hope. (March 19, 1978)

3. Jesus falls the first time.

Mark 8:34

Christ is not an insensitive man. Christ is a real person—of flesh and
bones, nerves and muscles, just like us. He is a man who feels just
like a person feels when he is carried away by the National Guard
and taken to a place of torture. (April 1, 1979)

4. Jesus meets his mother.

John 19:25–27

Brothers, the liberation of Christ is tenderness; it's love; it's the
presence of a loving mother, Mary. And Mary is the model of those
who collaborate with Christ for the liberation of the earth and the
acquisition of heaven. Mary, in her song of thanksgiving, proclaims

the greatness of God and also proclaims that God rejects the pride of the powerful and exalts the humble. (March 24, 1978)

5. Simon helps Jesus.

Luke 23:26

Unfortunately, dear brothers, we are the product of an education which is spiritualistic and individualistic, where we are taught "to gain salvation of the spirit, don't worry about others." Like we say to the suffering, "Have patience that you will get to heaven, endure!" No! That can't be. This isn't salvation, not the salvation that Christ brought. The salvation that Christ brings is the salvation from all the slaveries that oppress people. It is necessary that people break the chains that bind them: starting with the many oppression and slaveries, fears that enslave their hearts, illnesses that oppress their bodies, sadnesses, preoccupations, terrors that oppress their freedom and their life. (September 9, 1979)

6. Veronica wipes the face of Jesus.

Matthew 26:27

If we could see that Christ is the needy person, the tortured person, the prisoner, the murderer, the one thrown away with so much indignity on our roads. If we could discover in this rejected one Christ, we would treat this Christ as a medal of gold. We would pick him up with tenderness and kiss him. We would not feel ashamed of him. (March 16, 1980)

7. Jesus falls the second time.

John 12:24

Here, Christ is flesh that suffers. Here where Christ is something, he is persecution, where Christ is men who sleep out in the country because they can't sleep in their house, where Christ is sickness that suffers because of the consequences of being so unprotected. Here is Christ with the cross upon his shoulders on the road to Calvary, not meditated in some chapel with the way of the cross or lived outside the people. (March 5, 1978)

8. Jesus consoles the women.

Luke 23:27–28

The one who lives with the poor, the miserable, the peasant and who defends them and loves them like Christ our Lord, and who preaches the liberation of the poor, of the oppressed, of the one who suffers, this one is the Christ in our midst. (March 23, 1978)

9. Jesus falls for the third time.

Luke 17:1–2

No one is vanquished even though he is put under the boot of oppression and repression. He who believes in Christ knows that he is victor and that the ultimate victory will be from truth and from justice. (March 23, 1980, the day before his death)

How well Christ identified himself with the suffering of his people! Many shacks, many slums, many imprisoned by suffering, many hungry for justice and peace appear to clamor, "My God, my God, why have you abandoned me?" He hasn't abandoned us. This is the hour in which the Son of God is carrying all of the load of sins to obey God, asking him to pardon these sins of humanity from whom is derived all injustices, all selfishness. (April 8, 1979)

10. Jesus is stripped of his clothes.

John 19:23–24

This is the commitment of being a Christian: to follow Christ in his incarnation. And if Christ is a majestic God who becomes a humble man and lives with the poor until the death of slaves on a cross, our Christian faith should be lived in the same fashion. This Christian who doesn't want to live with this commitment of solidarity with the poor doesn't deserve to call himself a Christian. Christ invites us not to fear persecution because, believe it brothers, the one who binds himself with the poor has to go through the same destiny as the poor: to be disappeared, to be tortured, to be captured to appear as dead. (February 17, 1980)

11. Jesus is crucified.

Mark 15:22–25

Rome used to crucify people, but not Roman citizens. Rome used to crucify the people that depended on their empire. And since Palestine depended on Rome (Pilate was the representative of Rome to this oppressed people), Christ had to be humiliated like someone who didn't merit citizenship. (March 19, 1978)

12. Jesus dies on the cross.

Luke 23:44–46

While we look at Christ nailed to the cross, he invites us to discern from the sacred word a real mystery. If Christ is the representative for all people, we have to discover the suffering of our people in his suffering, his humiliation, his body scarred by the nails of the cross. This is our people tortured, crucified, spat upon, and humiliated for whom Christ our Lord is represented in order to give our very difficult situation a sense of redemption. (March 24, 1978)

13. Jesus is taken down from the cross.

Mark 15:43–46

Mary is the expression of the need of the Salvadoran people. Mary is the expression of the anguish of those who are in prison. Mary is the sadness of the mothers who have lost their children and no one will tell them where they are. Mary is the tenderness that looks with anguish for a solution. (December 24, 1978)

14. Jesus is buried.

John 19:42

Don't think, brothers, that our dead have left us. Their heaven, their eternal recompense, makes them more perfect in love. They are still loving the same causes that they died for. That means that in El Salvador this liberating force not only counts those who remain living, but also counts those who they wanted to kill who are more present than before in the people. (March 2, 1980)

PERMISSIONS

Chapter One

Page 2   From Kathryn Spink, *In the Silence of the Heart: Meditations by Mother Teresa of Calcutta and Her Co-workers* (London: SPCK, 1983). Used by permission.

Page 3   From Saint John Chrysostom, *More Prayers for PD Group Meetings.*

Page 4   From Linus Mundy, *A Man's Guide to Prayer* (New York: Crossroad, 1998), p. 73. Reprinted with permission.

Page 5   From Mother Teresa's reflection on the papal encyclical *The Mission of the Redeemer*. Copyright 2005 Missionaries of Charity Sisters c/o Mother Teresa of Calcutta Center. Used by permission.

Page 6   Reprinted with permission of Center of Concern, 1225 Otis Street, NE, Washington, DC 20017-2516. www.educationforjustice.org.

Page 7   From James R. Brockman, S.J., trans. and comp., *The Violence of Love: The Pastoral Wisdom of Archbishop Oscar Romero* (New York: Harper & Row, 1988), p. 118. Reprinted by permission of Chicago Province of the Society of Jesus and HarperCollins.

Page 8   From Lorraine Kisly, *Ordinary Graces* (New York: Random House, 2000). Used by permission of Bell Tower, a division of Random House, Inc.

Page 9   Excerpted from Carole Garibaldi Rogers and Mary Ann Jeselson, *The People's Prayer Book: Personal and Group Prayers* (Liguori, Mo.: Liguori, 2003). Used with permission of Liguori Publications, Liguori, MO 63057.

Page 10   Excerpt from *Sharing Catholic Social Teaching: Challenges and Directions* (Washington, D.C.: USCCB, 1999). Used with permission. All rights reserved.

Page 11	From the papal encyclical *Centesimus Annus*, 36.
Page 12	From *Francis of Assisi: Early Documents, Volume I: The Saint* (New York: New City Press, 1999) Used by permission of Franciscan Institute of St. Bonaventure, New York, New City Press, 202 Cardinal Road, Hyde Park, NY 12538 (www.newcitypress.com).
Page 13	From the Abbey of New Clairvaux, Viña, California.
Page 14	From George Appleton, ed., *The Oxford Book of Prayer* (Oxford: Oxford University Press, 2002).
Page 15	George Appleton, ed. *The Oxford Book of Prayer* (New York: Oxford University Press, 1985), p. 105.
Page 16	We gratefully acknowledge the authorship of Dr. Edward Francis Gabriele for these texts originally published in *Prayers with Searchers and Saints* (Winona, Minn.: Saint Mary's Press, 1998), pp. 112–115.

Chapter Two

Page 22	Dorothy Day from *The Long Loneliness*, Fritz Eichenberg, illus. (New York: Harper & Row, 1952), p. 285. Copyright renewed © 1980 by Tamar Teresa Hennessy. Reprinted by permission of HarperCollins Publishers.
Page 23	Many versions of Pastor Niemoller's poem have been circulated over the years. Some have added lines about Catholics and homosexuals or changed the order of victims. The text above is the original, as far as can be ascertained (http://www.serendipity.li/cda/niemoll.html).
Page 24	From Václav Havel, *Disturbing the Peace* (New York: Vintage Books, 1991).
Page 25	"A Prayer to the Holy Spirit" prayer card published by Pax Christi USA, 532 W. 8th Street, Erie, PA 16502. www.paxchristiusa.org. Reprinted with permission.
Page 26	From Monica Furlong, *Women Pray: Voices Through the Ages, from Many Faiths, Cultures and Traditions* (Woodstock, Vt.: Skylight Paths, 2001), p. 94. Permission granted by SkyLight Paths Publishing, P.O. Box 237, Woodstock, VT 05091 www.skylightpaths.com.
Page 27	From *Guidebook: Lay-Jesuit Year of Prayer* (Baltimore, Md.: Society of Jesus Maryland Province, 2005). Permission for publication granted by James L. Connor, s.j., Provincial Assistant for Mission and Renewal, Maryland Province, Society of Jesus.

Page 28	Helen Prejean, C.S.J., "A Prayer to Abolish the Death Penalty," prayer card published by Pax Christi, USA, 532 W. 8th Street, Erie, PA 16502. www.paxchristiusa.org. Reprinted with permission.
Page 29	Available at various sites on the Internet. Original source unknown.
Page 30	From Miriam Therese Winter, *WomanPrayer, WomanSong: Resources for Ritual* (New York: Crossroad, 1995). Reprinted with permission.
Page 32	Martin Luther King, Jr. *Where Do We Go From Here: Chaos or Community?* (New York: Harper & Row, 1967). Reprinted by arrangement with the Estate of Martin Luther King, Jr., c/o Writer's House as agent for the proprietor, New York, NY.
Pages 33–37	Reprinted with permission of the Center of Concern, 1225 Otis Street, NE, Washington, DC 20017-2516. www.educationforjustice.org.
Pages 38–46	We gratefully acknowledge the authorship of Dr. Edward Francis Gabriele for this text originally published in *Prayer with Searchers and Saints* (Winona, Minn.: Saint Mary's Press, 1998).

Chapter Three

Pages 48–51	Reprinted with permission by Interfaith Worker Justice, 1020 West Bryn Mawr, Chicago, IL 60660. For information about ordering multiple copies in bulletin-insert form, visit the IWJ web site at www.iwj.org.
Page 52	Reprinted with permission from *CRS Prayers without Borders: Celebrating Global Wisdom* Call 1-800-685-7572 to order.
Page 53	Cardinal John O'Connor, Labor Day Mass, St. Patrick's Cathedral, 1997. Reprinted from "The Rights of All," *Catholic New York*, September 11, 1997, p. 13.
Page 54	Reprinted with permission from *CRS Prayers without Borders: Celebrating Global Wisdom*. Call 1-800-685-7572 to order.
Page 55	Reprinted with permission of the Center of Concern, 1225 Otis Street, NE, Washington, DC 20017-2516. www.educationforjustice.org.
Page 56	Reprinted by permission of Most Rev. Jerome Hanus, O.S.B.
Pages 57–58	*Rural Life Prayerbook* (Des Moines, Iowa.: National Catholic Rural Life Conference, 1956). Reprinted with permission of National Catholic Rural Life Conference, 4625 Beaver Avenue, Des Moines, IA 50310. www.ncrlc.com.

Page 59   Reprinted with permission by Interfaith Worker Justice, 1020 West Bryn Mawr, Chicago, IL 60660. For information about ordering multiple copies in bulletin-insert form, visit the IWJ web site at www.iwj.org.

Chapter Four

Page 64   Henri Nouwen. *Compassion* (New York: Bantam Doubleday Dell, 1983). Used with permission of Random House, Inc.

Page 65   From George Appleton, ed., *The Oxford Book of Prayer* (Oxford: Oxford University Press, 2002).

Page 66   Reprinted with permission of Barbara Blossom. All rights reserved.

Page 67   Reprinted with permission of Jesuit Relief Services (Australia), P.O. Box 522 (24 Roslyn Street), Kings Cross NSW 1340, Australia.

Pages 68–71   Reprinted with permission of the Center of Concern, 1225 Otis Street, NE, Washington, D.C. 20017-2516. www.educationforjustice.org.

Page 72   Excerpted from Carole Garibaldi Rogers and Mary Ann Jeselson, *The People's Prayer Book: Personal and Group Prayers* (Liguori, Mo.: Liguori, 2003). Used with permission of Liguori Publications, Liguori, MO 63057.

Page 73   From *World Citizen News*, October, 1992. Reprinted with permission of NWO Publications, 113 Church Street, Burlington, VT 05401.

Page 74   The English translation of "Prayer of the Second Vatican Council" (Prayer for Meetings) from *A Book of Prayers* (Washington, D.C.: International Committee on English in the Liturgy, 1982). All rights reserved.

Pages 75–76   Reprinted with permission of the Center of Concern, 1225 Otis Street, NE, Washington, DC 20017-2516. www.educationforjustice.org.

Page 77   Excerpt from Kathleen Norris, *Dakota: A Spiritual Geography* (New York: Houghton Mifflin, 1993). Reprinted by permission. All rights reserved.

Page 78   We gratefully acknowledge the authorship of Dr. Edward Francis Gabriele for this text originally published in *Prayer with Searchers and Saints* (Winona, Minn.: Saint Mary's Press, 1998).

Chapter Five

Page 84   From Edwin Searcy, ed. *Awed to Heaven, Rooted in Earth: The Prayers of Walter Brueggemann* (Minneapolis: Augsburg Fortress, 2003). Used by permission.

Page 86   "A Prayer for Global Restoration," written by Michelle Balek, O.S.F. Published as a prayer card by Pax Christi, USA, 532 W. 8th Street, Erie, PA 16502, www.paxchristi.org. Reprinted with permission.

Page 88   Reprinted with permission of the diocese of Sioux Falls.

Page 90   From Lorie Simmons, comp. and ed., *Come Holy Spirit* (Chicago: Liturgy Training Publications, 2001), p. 28.

Page 91   From Lorraine Kisly, *Ordinary Graces* (New York: Random House, 2000). Used by permission of Bell Tower, a division of Random House, Inc.

Page 92   From Thomas McNally, C.S.C. and William G. Storey, D.M.S., eds., *Lord Hear Our Prayer* (Notre Dame, Ind.: Ave Maria, 2000). Used with permission of Ave Maria Press, P.O. Box 428, Notre Dame, IN 46556, www.avemariapress.com.

Page 94   Reprinted from *Peace with God the Creator, Peace with All Creation* (Washington, D.C.: USCCB, 1995).

Page 96   From Elizabeth Roberts, *Earth Prayers from Around the World* (San Francisco: HarperSanFrancisco, 1991).

Chapter Six

Page 98   Copyright © Satish Kumar, editor of *Resurgence*, www.resurgence.org. First published in *In the Silence of the Heart: Meditations by Mother Teresa of Calcutta and Her Co-workers* (London: SPCK, 1983).

Page 99   Adapted from traditional prayer.

Page 100   Used by permission of Africa Action, www.africaaction.org.

Page 102   From James R. Brockman, S.J., trans. and comp., *The Violence of Love: The Pastoral Wisdom of Archbishop Oscar Romero* (New York: Harper & Row, 1988), p. 100. Reprinted by permission of Chicago Province of the Society of Jesus and HarperCollins.

Page 103   From *The War Prayer*, dictated by Mark Twain in 1905. First published in *Harper's Monthly*, November, 1916.

Page 104   From Gabe Huck, Vicky Tufano and Lorie Simmons, eds., *Grant Us Peace* (Chicago: Liturgy Training Publications, 1991, 2002).

Page 105   From Edwin Searcy, ed., *Awed to Heaven, Rooted in Earth: The Prayers of Walter Brueggemann* (Minneapolis: Augsburg Fortress, 2003). Used by permission.

Page 107 — Joan D. Chittister, O.S.B. "Prayer for World Peace," prayer card published by Pax Christi USA, 532 W. 8th Street, Erie, PA 16502. www.paxchristiusa.org. Reprinted with permission.

Page 109 — Reprinted with permission of the Center of Concern, 1225 Otis Street, NE, Washington, D.C. 20017-2516. www.educationforjustice.org.

Page 110 — Reprinted with permission of John Dear, S.J., www.johndear.org.

Page 112 — Copyright 2003 Marianne Hieb, R.S.M., Sisters of Mercy of the Americas. www.puddinghouse.com (Peacelines). Reprinted with permission of the author.

Page 114 — From Ellen Bass, *The Human Line* (Port Townsend, Wash.: Copper Canyon Press, 2007). Originally published in *The Sun*, June, 2003, p. 47. Reprinted with permission of Ellen Bass, www.ellenbass.com.

Page 117 — Prayer card published by Pax Christi, USA, 532 W 8th Street, Erie, PA 16502.

Page 118 — "Litany of Mary of Nazareth" prayer card published by Pax Christi USA, 532 W. 8th Street, Erie, PA 16502. www.paxchristiusa.org. Reprinted with permission.

Page 120 — John Dear, S.J., *The Sound of Listening: A Retreat Journal from Thomas Merton's Hermitage* (New York: Continuum Books, 1999). Reprinted with permission of John Dear, S.J., www.johndear.org, and the Continuum International Publishing Group.

Chapter Seven

Page 128 — This prayer is often mistakenly attributed to Archbishop Oscar Romero. It was written for Cardinal John Dearden by Bishop Kenneth Untener for a November, 1979, Mass honoring deceased priests. The full details of Untener's authorship of the prayer were revealed by Detroit Auxiliary Bishop Thomas Gumbleton in his March 28, 2004 *National Catholic Reporter* column, "The Peace Pulpit." Reprinted with permission of the diocese of Saginaw.

Page 129 — Reprinted with permission of the National Pastoral Life Center. Prayer cards available from NPLC, 18 Bleecker Street, New York, NY 10012.

Page 130 — Cardinal John Newman, "Hope in God-Creator," *Meditations on Christian Doctrine*, March 7, 1848.

Page 131 — From Gabe Huck, Vicky Tufano and Lorie Simmons, eds., *Grant Us Peace* (Chicago: Liturgy Training Publications, 1991, 2002).

Page 132	From Ronald Rolheiser *The Holy Longing: The Search for a Christian Spirituality* (New York: Doubleday, 1998), p. 73. Used by permission of Doubleday, a division of Random House, Inc.
Page 133	Excerpt from Msgr. Geno C. Baroni's last homily from the Mass card for his funeral.
Page 134	Reprinted with permission of the Center of Concern, 1225 Otis Street, NE, Washington, D.C. 20017-2516. www.educationforjustice.org.
Page 135	Excerpt from *Communities of Salt and Light: Parish Resource Manual* (Washington, D.C.: USCCB, 1994). Used with permission. All rights reserved.
Page 136	From Edwin Searcy, ed. *Awed to Heaven, Rooted in Earth: The Prayers of Walter Brueggemann* (Minneapolis: Augsburg Fortress, 2003).
Page 138	Archbishop Dom Helder Camara. *The Desert Is Fertile* (Maryknoll, N.Y.: Orbis, 1974). Reprinted with permission of Orbis Books.
Page 139	Copyright © 1956, 1958 by the Abbey of Our Lady of Gethsemani. Reprinted by permission of Curtis Brown, Ltd.
Page 140	From *Mil Voces Para Celebrar* (Nashville: United Methodist Publishing House, 1996). Reprinted by permission of Abington Press.
Pages 142–143	From Lorie Simmons, ed., *Come Holy Spirit* (Chicago: Liturgy Training Publications, 2001).
Page 144	From Janet Morley, ed., *Bread of Tomorrow: Prayers for the Church Year* (Maryknoll, N.Y.: Orbis, 1992).
Page 145	From *Proclaim Praise: Daily Prayer for Parish and Home* (Chicago: Liturgy Training Publications, 1995). Reprinted with permission Liturgy Training Publications, 1800 N. Hermitage Ave., Chicago, IL 60622.
Page 147	From *Wee Worship Book* (Glasgow: Wild Goose, n.d.) Reprinted with permission of Wild Goose Publications, Iona Community, Fourth Floor, Savoy House, 140 Sauchiehall Street, Glasgow G2 3DH, Scotland.
Page 148	Reprinted with permission of Jeff Dols.
Page 149	From James R. Brockman, S.J., trans. and comp., *The Violence of Love: The Pastoral Wisdom of Archbishop Oscar Romero* (New York: Harper & Row, 1988), pp. 39–40. Reprinted by permission of Chicago Province of the Society of Jesus and HarperCollins.
Page 150	From Ronald Rolheiser, *The Holy Longing: The Search for a Christian Spirituality* (New York: Doubleday, 1998). Used by permission of Doubleday, a division of Random House, Inc.

Page 151	From Macrina Wiederkehr, O.S.B., "Morning Prayer," *Seasons of Your Heart* (New York: HarperCollins, 1991). Reprinted with permission.
Page 152	Used with the permission of the Maryknoll Sisters, Maryknoll, NY 10545.
Page 154	Linus Mundy, *A Man's Guide to Prayer* (New York: Crossroad, 1998), p. 42. Reprinted with permission.
Page 155	Adapted from Rabbi Jack Riemer, "Social Action," *Kol Haneshemah: Shabbat Vehagim* (Elkins Park, Penn.: The Reconstructionist Press, 1994).

Chapter Eight

Page 158	From Howard Thurman *The Mood of Christmas* (Richmond, Ind.: Friends United, 1985). Used by permission.
Page 159	From Richard J. Beyer, *Blessed Art Thou* (Notre Dame, Ind.: Ave Maria Press, 1996). Used by permission.
Page 160	Sisters of Mercy Mid-Atlantic Justice Office, December 1995. Reprinted with permission of Sisters of Mercy of the Americas. www.sistersofmercy.org/justice/election_prayer.html. All rights reserved.
Page 161	Reprinted with permission from *CRS Prayers without Borders: Celebrating Global Wisdom*, call 1-800-685-7572 to order.
Page 162	Reprinted with permission of the Center of Concern, 1225 Otis Street, NE, Washington, D.C. 20017-2516. www.educationforjustice.org.
Page 163	Jan L. Richardson, *Sacred Journeys: A Woman's Book of Daily Prayer* (Nashville: Upper Room Books, 1995). Used with permission.
Page 165	Reprinted with permission of the Center of Concern, 1225 Otis Street, NE, Washington, D.C. 20017-2516. www.educationforjustice.org.

Chapter Nine

| Page 168 | We gratefully acknowledge the authorship of Dr. Edward Francis Gabriele for these texts originally published in *Prayers with Searchers and Saints* (Winona, Minn.: Saint Mary's Press, 1998). |
| Page 174 | From *The Worshipbook* (Louisville, Ky.: Westminster John Knox, 1972). Reprinted with permission of Westminster John Knox Press. All rights reserved. |

Page 177   Adapted from the *New Revised Standard Version Bible*, copyright © 1989, Division of Christian Education of the National Council of Churches in Christ in the United States of America.

Page 178   Prayer Service, copyright Catholic Diocese of Richmond. Used with permission. Prayers are excerpts from *Sharing Catholic Social Teaching: Challenges and Directions* (Washington, D.C.: USCCB, 1999). Used with permission. All rights reserved.

Page 181   Reprinted with permission of The Fellowship of Reconciliation, Box 271, Nyack NY 10960.

Page 183   From Ronald Rolheiser, *The Holy Longing: The Search for a Christian Spirituality* (New York: Doubleday, 1998). Used by permission of Doubleday, a division of Random House, Inc.

Pages 185–194   Reprinted with permission of the Center of Concern, 1225 Otis Street, NE, Washington, D.C. 20017-2516. www.educationforjustice.org.

Page 195   From *Monseñnor Romero: El Pueblo Es Mi Profeta* (San Salvador: Equipo de Educacion Maiz, 1994). Reprinted by permission of the publisher.

INDEX OF AUTHORS

INDEX OF TITLES